Rebuild, Reset & Recover

7 Steps to Spiritual Abuse Recovery

By Mercy Myles-Jenkins

Copyright © 2020 by Mercy Myles-Jenkins

All rights reserved. This book or any portion thereof may not be reproduced or used in any manner whatsoever without the express written permission of the publisher except for the use of brief quotations in a book review.

All scripture quotations, unless otherwise indicated, are taken from the NEW KING JAMES VERSION®. Copyright© 1982 by Thomas Nelson, Inc.

Used by permission. All rights reserved

Printed in the United States of America

First Printing, 2020

ISBN: 9798677595578

Edited & Formatted by Show Your Success

Published by Mercy Myles-Jenkins

Dedication

I dedicate this book to my husband Aaron, my children Ashanti, Kimani, Isaiah, Destin and Levi, my siblings, nephews and nieces. I love and appreciate you all, for allowing me to fight to produce book after book without complaint. This means a lot to me. May God continue to bless each of you.

Acknowledgments

Firstly I want to acknowledge my Heavenly Father for pushing me forward. I am so humbled by Holy Spirit inspiring and directing me to add another book to now a series of 5 books on Spiritual Abuse. In a midst of a pandemic, He unctioned me not to just write but to empower others to write, publish and launch too. This part I had never seen!

I would like to thank my leaders for participating in the construction of this book from the foreword by Apostle Elizabeth Hairston-McBurrows, and a chapter by my Pastor Prophetess Dawn Akita Wellington.

Thank you to Myria Thompson for working with me. Your readiness encourages me to keep going!

I am forever grateful to those who trust me to lead them as a pastor, my Christ Church International Springfield family, and those I lead in the capacity of a mentor and coach.

Thank you for giving me the privilege to lead you as Christ leads me.

I want to acknowledge those who have experienced spiritual abuse to let you know that you are not forgotten. God has heard your cry, and it is on His agenda to set you free! I am grateful for the life lessons that this experience has given me, especially as I am now a part of

Acknowledgments

that church leadership. My prayer for you is that God will continue to strengthen and uplift you to do great exploits for Him!

I would like to especially thank the following individuals who supported me and bought a copy of this book on pre-sale:

Name	From Email Address
Author Pamela Garrison	gorgeousgarrison@gmail.com
Susan Barclay	terrysue051@gmail.com
Divine Identity Christian Coaching & Consulting	divineid3@gmail.com
Little Angels Bible Academy	littleangelsba@yahoo.co.uk
Leandria Benton	treetunk@q.com
Sharice Paulemon	sharjohnson22@yahoo.com
Jerrica Brumfield	info@jerricabrumfield.com
Five Fold Publishing	reverendrita@5foldpublishing.com
True Sound School of Music	truesoundschoolofmusic@yahoo.com
Kimbely Williams	princess4901@yahoo.com
Corinne Lawrence	corinnelawrence1@gmail.com
Linda Neal	jettasunshine@comcast.net
Danysia Thompson	danysialaurin@gmail.com
Together We Agree	twaministry@gmail.com
The Family Circle, Inc.	thefamilycircle01@yahoo.com
Afri (K)que Limited	kar_tess@yahoo.fr
Joy Jenkins	joys4boyz@gmail.com
Cassandra S Pickett	cassandrapickett@yahoo.com
Flaming Heart Ministries	tina@flamingheartministries.org

Acknowledgments

WFG/Rebecca	becky.wfg45@gmail.com
Stephens Enterprises	thankgod43@gmail.com
Candace Joyner	iwillpursue@gmail.com
Jennifer Bratcher	jlbratch23@gmail.com
Gionne Ralph	gionne.jonesralph@gmail.com
Rhonda Jones	boorhonda@hotmail.com
Tara Henry	tara.henry09@gmail.com
Yamesha Davis	yamesha.davis@yahoo.com
Cassandra Elliott Ministries	info@thewlmn.com
Lavern Green	gogrgreen@aol.com
Sherlene Taylor	cheeseheadnum1@gmail.com
Yrene Ekwayolo	elikiyajoy@gmail.com
Blake Shaw	b.shaw777@yahoo.com
Joyce Ann Thompson	jthomp3256@comcast.net
Maxine Collins	mmxcollins@aol.com
Pamela Hillsman	min.peh2013@gmail.com
Sonji Williams	swdw25@yahoo.com
Sam Thompson	samlynettethompson@sbcglobal.net
Darius Taylor	darius.t1914@gmail.com
Juliet Bernard	julietbernard68@gmail.com
Cathy Kerner	mckerners@gmail.com
Academic Associates	mdthomp3921@gmail.com
Cathy Busari	
Makeba Hart	fastclosingskansascity@gmail.com
Stephanie Romero	
Mershelia Williams	
Queen Nicole	
Mamie Cameron	
Nicole McNair	

Acknowledgments

Rhonda Walla

Beverly George

Sonya Hurt Ministries

Deborah L. Anderson

Georgia Lue

Apostle

Hairston-McBurrows

Marshawn Kerner

Shana Bana

About the Author

Mercy Myles-Jenkins was born and raised in London, England, by Ghanaian parentage. She currently resides in Massachusetts with her family.

Mercy is an ordained pastor of Christ Church International Springfield, an apostolic-prophetic church. Mercy believes that the restoration of your spiritual health is self-care and encourages the church to support this forgotten group.

Mercy is a certified Life Coach and supports women to overcome spiritual abuse through coaching. Mercy has written 5 books on overcoming Spiritual Abuse and in that process, she became a Book Coach with a successful Book Coaching program. Mercy started her company Legacy Driven Consulting & Publishing, as a mission to inspire and equip women to build their legacy by leading with their story in a book. Mercy empowers women to emerge from being invisible to evolve, as they learn to find their voice to make an impact.

Other Books by Mercy Myles-Jenkins

God's Mercy in the Wilderness: Finding Your Calling & Purpose in the Midst of Church Hurt

Run for Your Life! Freedom from Spiritual Abuse & Lessons Learned

Mercy Speaks: A Collection of Poems - Intimate Thoughts, Prayers and Self-Reflection

Uncovering the Betrayal of Spiritual Abuse

Mercy
MYLES-JENKINS
Author/Speaker/Real Estate Investor
Grab Your Copy Today!
Tel: (413) 351-8154
Purpose Pusher
President: New England Branch,
Women With A Call International
www.CoachMercyMylesJenkins.com

Foreword

Mercy Myles-Jenkins has greatly penned 7 Steps of Spiritual Abuse Recovery, a book that is needed for individuals who have experienced domestic or spiritual abuse.

The similarities are that of trauma but the recovery process is different in some way.

This book has not been written for entertainment but solely for information, and is designed to bring about transformation because, deliverance from abuse will become evident as the reader follows the Seven Steps properly and applies them at this juncture of their lives.

Elizabeth Hairston-McBurrows, DMIN, DBS, PhD

7 Steps of Spiritual Abuse Recovery

Chapter 1	Step 1 Repossess - Regaining Back Your Power	1
Chapter 2	Step 2 Retrieve - Replace and Release	7
Chapter 3	Step 3 Reset - Reclaim Your Identity	17
Chapter 4	Step 4 Rebuild - Rebuilding You!	31
Chapter 5	Step 5 Re-establish a New Life	55
Chapter 6	Step 6 Revive – Re-Awakening the Spiritual Giant Within	63
Chapter 7	Step 7 - Recover - Making a Full Recovery	75
Chapter 8	More than a Conqueror by Myria Thompson	87
Chapter 9	Overcomer's Written Interviews	95

A Special Note to Pastors

Dear Pastor,

Thank you for reading this book. I pray that it has been an eye-opener for you. My prayer is that it will help to equip you with more in-depth knowledge and understanding on how to care for those who visit and or become members in your church, who come to you for healing and restoration from being spiritually abused. I believe that total restoration occurs when a person returns to God and finds a new church home. Once attending a church, the challenges they will face is to trust leadership again. With your support and understanding, their time in the wilderness, wondering could be reduced as your church provides them a stable spiritual home.

    I also hope that this insight will cause leaders to develop best practices and protocols to steer other leaders away from abusing their position. I trust that it will also be a resource for you and your leadership to cultivate the heart of a servant leader to carry a burden to be compassionate towards the people as did Jesus.

    I want to honor and thank you for sacrificing your lives for the sake of those whom you are called to serve. The work that we do is both challenging and rewarding. I want to encourage you to keep standing firm in your

A Special Note to Pastors

calling and assignment, regardless of those who preach the gospel for wrong motives. God sees you, and we appreciate you very much!

Kingdom Blessings!

Pastor Mercy

P.S.
My gift to you is the framework/assessment tool for the 7 Steps to Spiritual Abuse Recovery, in an infograph. Get it NOW!: www.rebuildbonus.com

Background

This book is about realizing that your spiritual health has been injured by narcissistic leadership that has strong-armed you into relinquishing your personal power to being manipulated, controlled, dominated, and brainwashed by them for selfish gain. Narcissists as church leaders, operate by creating a church culture that binds their members to religious obligations by systematic fear embedded in its doctrines, teachings, communications, and expectations.

Most people would call out such leaders as 'Jezebelic Leadership' or 'Charismatic Witchcraft,' 'Cults.' It's all of those things. I choose to refer to it as spiritual abuse and not 'church hurt'. The reason being is because it emphasizes the church unfairly and not the behavior. For example, children who are abused at school are bullied, but we don't term that school hurt. This principle does not apply to the workplace, family, or in a club. These are all places that we experience hurt, abuse, and trauma, but we do not connect the hurt to the situation but an individual.

The other reason is that the Holy Spirit checked me on the use of 'church hurt.' Through the word, He explained to me that we unfairly sling mud on His Bride when Jesus Christ died for the church and purchased it with his blood,

Background

Acts 20:28 says,

> "Therefore take heed to yourselves and to all the flock, among which the Holy Spirit has made you overseers, to shepherd the Church of God which **He purchased with His own blood**."

Spiritual abuse refers to the use of religious principles, biblical doctrines, and abuse of church leadership authority and power used to control, manipulate, and dominate its members.

Ultimately, we know the source of spiritual abuse is demonic and is assigned to destroy people's lives and their faith in God and His ways. Throughout this book I also use the words 'controlling church' and 'cultic church' and 'cultic church culture' interchangeably, to mean the same thing.

This book marks my fifth book on this matter and gives little detail into my personal account. For more on my personal testimony, you can read about it in the book titled 'Run For Your Life.'

Recovery is the process of what it means to recover. While we are fit and healthy, we rarely pay attention to the benefits of having limbs. It is when we are injured and in need of surgery that we realize how vital our health is.

Medical professionals create care plans for their patient's recovery and prescribe treatment and a timeline for recovery. Understanding the process of healing

Background

and how to manage it is very important to the success of the recovery process. This is my intention for writing the book. That you will be able to analyse and glean from the seven steps of spiritual abuse recovery to guage where you are in the healing process and to be proactive in accepting help to overcome and to be spiritually restored.

My goal is to educate and empower you to rebuild your life despite the challenges that you have experienced. You are valuable and have a lot to contribute in this world. This book is a reminder that it is now time to reset, recover, and rebuild as I share with you seven steps to recover from spiritual abuse.

CHAPTER 1

Step 1: Repossess & Regain Back your Power

> Your first step to recovery is to **regain re-possession of your life** by removing yourself from the abuser. Without doing this, you cannot heal and recover. If you are in an abusive relationship, the healing occurs as you depart from them.

According to Merriam Webster's Dictionary, the word repossess is defined as a judicial process to take back goods to the original owner when the agreement is broken.

This is a noteworthy word in understanding that you first belong to God. If you are treated in an ungodly manner by God's delegated leadership, there is a process that the original owner can claim you back. God did not intend for your soul to be possessed by man. His intent is that shepherds lead and oversee the souls of man according to his heart (1 Peter 2:25 and Jeremiah 3:15).

Step 1: Repossess & Regain Back your Power

Needy People Need to be Needed

In an abusive relationship, the first thing is to sever ties and get out. It would appear to be the most natural part, but it is not. First of all, you may incline that something is wrong. However, your desire to see the best in people may have you making excuses for abusive behavior. On the outside, everything looks good, but you feel awkward, coerced, fearful, anxious, and confused inside. Somehow things are not making sense to you. In trying to make sense of things, you ponder about speaking to your pastor to ask a question, but that would be questioning his motive and would cause you to look like you are rebellious and non-conforming. You have seen what happens to people that go this route, and so you decide that it is not worth rocking the boat as it is too costly on your self-esteem to be rebuked publicly and placed in quarantine by the church.

In this type of church culture, your ability to conform is what will cost you your life. It's the ingredient that causes you to lose the essence of who you are as a person. The more involved you are in this cultic church culture, the more you will become a zombie, like the rest of them under the control of a correctional officer. Zombie life is all about being spiritually dead. This culture removes individuality and sees it as a threat to the leader's governing authority over its organization.

Step 1: Repossess & Regain Back your Power

In my book 'Run For Your Life', there is a section on a prophetic dream I had of zombies. This dream was the spark that ignited me to leave this type of organization. Without the dream enlightening me, it would have been difficult to go as I had already invested years into this church. But God had enough as it was killing the destiny that He had planned for my life.

Many people find it difficult to leave these types of controlling church cultures and often, find a way of returning to fulfill a void within themselves. The narcissistic leader has a magnetic pull on their members. The pull works through the church programming, and the members need to be loved, accepted and validated. Those who don't suffer rejection issues will move on without a flinch. Narcissistic leaders will release them because they cannot control them. The game is over because they have lost control over that person. If you suffer from unresolved issues from childhood and low self-esteem, you are vulnerable and needed by the leader to build their dictatorial regime. The fact that you feel needed is how you are baited into their trap. Needy people need to be needed and a regime like this provides that for them. Almost like providing you your drug, an insatiable need for a sense of security and identity. Once you understand this, then you can recover all!

Step 1: Repossess & Regain Back your Power

Run For Your Life and Leave The Church!

Telling people to leave their church is controversial. We certainly do not want people in the body of Christ to be displaced or encouraged to church hop around. Neither do we want to be seen as sowing cords of dissension by telling people to leave a church. However, we should know that this is not the case with a cultic church. We must be bold enough to speak the truth and set the captives free from such churches.

Here is a list of reasons to leave a church:

- Churches requires you to take a ritual bath
- Have sex for favors e.g. prayer
- Mandated systematically to do things against your personal will
- To participate in inhumane and illegal behavior
- To be intimate with other members
- To allow adults to have unsupervised time with your children
- Dictate relationships within the family and the outside world
- Sow seeds of mistrust with everyone but not with the leader
- Driven to worship the leader
- Focus heavily on mandatory rules and religious obligations to the church

Step 1: Repossess & Regain Back your Power

The list above is not a church but a prison, a gang, if you will. It does not represent the heart and mind of Christ. This is not a church to try and work things out and hope for a better future. These leaders walk in pride and will not back down or repent. That's why you must leave! It's time out for lives shipwrecked and destinies hijacked by these charlatans!

It is time to take back your life and get free from such a church. Don't go back there under any circumstances; it is a sure thing that they will drag you back in again if you give them a chance. This even means that you cannot be in communication with those in the church who do not see what you see. Leave them alone; you cannot rescue everybody. You and your immediate family must leave. I have heard of several cases whereby the couple would split up over this, and one would go and one would stay behind. This is heartbreaking! The church should not be more important than a marriage.

Just like in domestic violence relationships, there are incidences where you must use tact to leave. That could mean you don't tell anyone at all, not even the pastor. Listen, I believe in leaving a church in order. It's always good practice to first meet with the pastor, releasing any responsibilities and items belonging to the church, training your replacement, blessing the leadership with a card, seed and gift. But in some of these churches, if you did all of that, you could be killed physically or spiritually. I have heard of people invited to eat a meal after their leaving

Step 1: Repossess & Regain Back your Power

announcement, and they just knew it was contaminated poison to bring them in a spiritual agreement and demonic impartation all over again and with a curse of sickness.

The first step to recovery is to gain Re-Possession of your life by removing yourself from the abuser. Without doing this, you cannot heal and recover. If you are in a relationship being battered and bruised mentally and spiritually, the healing occurs as you depart from them.

Don't believe the lie that if you stay, they will change. Narcissists do not change; they cannot feel the pain that they inflict upon you. Yes! They are charming and seemingly caring individuals but all with a purpose to control and deceive you with their lies and deceptive ways. They have studied their craft to control and dominate and will not let go, for it brings them much gain. Believe it or not, they have insecurities, and so you worshipping them fulfills their cry....Sound familiar? There is only one God, and He deserves all of your worship, but these leaders have created a system of stealing God's people and His Glory to be worshipped by the people.

Chapter 2

Step 2: Retrieve & Replace

> What was stored on the hard drive of your mind by the controlling church was erroneous and toxic. Your willingness to allow truth to minister and correct what you have been taught will begin the process of replacing unsound doctrine and religious biases when reading the Bible. In this process, you will unlearn and re-learn the true heart of the Father. You will begin to see the imbalance of issues that were emphasized as issues of salvation when they are not.

Merriam Webster's Dictionary Dictionary defines retrieve as 1) a means to correct and to issue a remedy for evil consequences 2) to call to mind again and 3) to recover from storage.

Now that you have decided to break ties with the abusive church, **step 2 is to retrieve and replace.** The Bible tells us in Acts 17:28 *"It is in Christ that for in we live and move and have our being."* In other words, we exist because of Him, and it is He that empowers us to live a life that glorifies Him. The mind is the storehouse of memories and information; it is why the Bible tells us in I Corinthians 2:16 "Who has known the mind of the LORD that he may instruct Him?" As a Christian you can develop the mind of Christ by studying the Bible. Then you will be able to walk in the instruction of the Lord. This will help you to remedy harmful information that was seeded in your mind. Once you have corrected and remedied erroneous words, practices, and ideas, you will replace them with the word of God to re-establish a righteous foundation to move forward and build.

Retrieve Hidden Truths to Replace Doctrinal Errors

To recover from spiritual abuse, one of the things that you must do is recognize what you had experienced through retrieving information outside of the organization. Listening to the counsel of loved ones or other pastors in different churches will ignite you to seek out new information to challenge what you have stored. **What was stored on the hard drive of your mind by the controlling church was erroneous and toxic. Your willingness to allow truth to minister and correct what you have been taught will begin the process of replacing unsound doctrine and religious biases when reading the Bible. In this process, you will unlearn and re-learn the true heart of the Father. You**

Step 2: Retrieve & Replace

will begin to see the imbalance of issues that were emphasized as issues of salvation when they are not.

When I came out of this whole episode, I went to the library and read seven books on Cults. I felt like it was important to understand and be knowledgeable in order to heal and help other's to overcome from their ordeal. I found out that most people that leave have a tendency to go back to that organization. and so it is essential to understand and have an awareness of your issues that attract you like a magnet for abuse.

Familiar Triggers for Abuse

You may have noticed a pattern with your family upbringing and choice of partners. For instance, maybe you were raised in a home of 'yelling parents.' Which allowed you to be accustomed to verbal abuse from people that yelled to change your personality, making you feel like you're not good enough. Driving you to be a people-pleaser, harboring rejection and formed habits to self-sabotage your success. **Spiritual abusive leaders cause a deep sense of betrayal that traumatizes your belief system and your faith in God and His people.**

I want to help you to recognize these triggers to identify where they've come from so that you never have to relive these experiences again unnecessarily. Not that you can stop these things from happening, but you can choose not to participate.

Step 2: Retrieve & Replace

In retrieving hidden information, we have to ask lots of questions and have a curiosity to know the truth.

Reflective Questions:

- Have you noticed that when somebody asks you to do something, it is difficult for you to say no?
- Have you noticed a disposition to please spiritual leadership even when the request does not align with the Bible or moral values?
- Do you change your opinions in a group when others have spoken up?
- Are you afraid to speak your mind?
- Do you have a hard time valuing your thoughts, your beliefs, hunches, and your discernment?

If you said yes to these questions, I want you to ask yourself why and where does this come from?

You may have realized through this reflective exercise that your sense of self is wounded and trapped. Now that you can see this, you are on the journey to heal, restore, and rebuild. I am proud of you for walking this journey. It's not an easy one, but it is worth it, and you are worth every moment that it takes to heal your wounds. Now I'm not a therapist, so here goes my disclaimer. I have gone through this experience with guidance from the Holy Spirit. I have overcome the abuse, the betrayal of the hurt, and have rebuilt my life and restored a fractured destiny.

Step 2: Retrieve & Replace

Here is a list of triggers that invite abusive behaviors like a magnet:
- ❑ Walking in fear
- ❑ Afraid to speak up
- ❑ Feelings of shame
- ❑ I don't like myself
- ❑ I'm different and would rather fit in
- ❑ Victim mentality
- ❑ The world doesn't understand me
- ❑ I feel lonely inside
- ❑ Everybody else has a better life than me
- ❑ Suicidal thoughts
- ❑ Experiencing a crisis
- ❑ Emotionally traumatized
- ❑ PTSD
- ❑ Depression
- ❑ People pleaser
- ❑ Seeking validation
- ❑ Woe is me syndrome
- ❑ Self-pity
- ❑ Feelings of powerlessness
- ❑ I have no rights
- ❑ Feelings of inferiority; you're better than me
- ❑ I have nothing to give, no value
- ❑ I don't know why they like me
- ❑ Feelings of insecurity
- ❑ An unstable life
- ❑ No motivation for life

Step 2: Retrieve & Replace

Wiping the Slate Clean: Forgive and Let Go!

Now that you have gained some insight, you have figured out how people can take advantage of you. You have realized that there are triggers that are like sound waves calling abusers from far to torment you to make your life a misery. But the devil is a liar! Jesus said, *"I have come to give you life and to give you life more abundantly"* (John 10:10). This is where your abundant life begins. Because you have flipped the narrative, your life story is now one of abundance and redemption.

The days where you were feeling bored, lonely, and lacked motivation are now in the past. You can move forward now to work on your self-esteem, self-confidence, and self-worth. To do this, we're first going to forgive. You need to forgive yourself for not sticking up for you. You are going to forgive the abuser, not to justify their behavior, but because you understand your life has been in a holding bay for too long. You are going to forgive and release them out of your heart so that you can move on. Also, you forgive, so you also will be forgiven (Matthew 6:14-15).

In some cases, you also have to forgive those who worked alongside the abusive leader when, for instance, it could be a whole church family instead of one individual.

And lastly, you need to forgive God. Sometimes it's hard to know that God was right there all along and saw

Step 2: Retrieve & Replace

what had happened to you. In my journey, when I left that church, I made a complaint to God about my treatment there. He brought it back to my remembrance all the time that he had sent people to open up my eyes to see the truth. But because of my issues, I was biased and was unable to see the truth of what was happening to me. This set me free because I realized that God is love and He did reach out to me several times, and in fact, He sent me a warning before it got even worse. It was my nature to overlook the red flags because I knew I was not perfect and wanted to be understood and accepted for my own mistakes and personality flaws. I was looking for self-acceptance and approval to feel liked. My personal needs kept me trapped, and I found it hard to escape at the time.

Psalm 124:7 says,

"Our soul has escaped as a bird from the snare of the fowlers; The snare is broken, and we have escaped".

Proverbs 6:5 says,

"Free yourself, like a gazelle from the hand of the hunter, like a bird from the fowler's snare."

At times we try to shift the blame on God or somebody else. But this proverb reminds us that we must free ourselves and fight our way to escape from bondage.

Step 2: Retrieve & Replace

I want you to be aware that soul ties must be broken. The entrapment happens in your soul, mind, your will, and emotions. To go through the process of forgiveness, you will also have to pray for yourself and cancel any and every emotional connection, agreement, and contract of unfulfilled expectations, to truly be free.

Below is a step-by-step prayer to guide you through to be set free.

Prayer For Forgiveness

If you are facing these challenges, you have to pray for your deliverance to breakthrough. Pray wholeheartedly for:

1. Pray and repent for holding any offence, rejection, anger, and mistrust in your heart.
2. Pray for a clean break from the inner vows you have made that prevented you from developing relationships with the church folk, church leadership, and God.
3. Pray for forgiveness for not trusting in God and for believing in man. The ability to forgive and release those who have hurt you. Call out their names.
4. Decree and declare yourself divorced from all contracts, written and unwritten with spiritual darkness and wickedness.

Step 2: Retrieve & Replace

5. Decree and declare your commitment to your Lord Jesus Christ, your Savior.
6. Denounce, renounce, and break any and every false religion, false doctrine, and false prophetic words by which you are bound.
7. Break and sever any and every ungodly soul ties that are blocking you from fulfilling your purpose and calling. (Virkler & Virkler, p 2001).

I would encourage you to read the following books; they helped me to understand the spiritual implications, spiritual abuse had on the condition of my heart and how to pray for healing and deliverance. Prayers that Heal the Heart by Mark and Patti Virkler and Prayers that Rout out Demons by Apostle John Eckhardt.

RECOUP: Time is a Healer, and So Is Effective Prayer!

This is your time to heal your inner self. It takes time to heal, so don't feel bad if you feel like you are still dealing with issues of anger, resentment, guilt, shame and embarrassment, hatred, and bitterness. Trust that God is still working on you to pull things out of your heart. It might be happening at a slower pace than what you expect but remember you experienced trauma and you need time to recoup. This is just the beginning of your recovery journey. I was stuck in negative feelings for five

Step 2: Retrieve & Replace

and a half years. Hopefully, this won't be you. I remember I would spew out mess out of my mouth every time I heard someone talk about church. Crazy, I know, but I was trying to find my place and voice. It took the prayers of those around me to pray me out of this traumatic experience even though outwardly, everything seemed normal.

Using your authority and spiritual weapons in prayer will ensure your freedom. Allow the Holy Spirit to guide you as He can also reveal to you things that you did not know about that would be essential to cancel, revoke, renounce, and denounce. When we fight for our freedom, it is a time of spiritual warfare. Don't give up on the life that you are worthy of having!

If you find yourself struggling to move forward, then I want to encourage you to seek professional counseling, pastoral counseling, or even life coaching to support your journey. Just so that you know, I provide coaching that supports the rebuilding of life and faith.

CHAPTER 3

Step 3: Reset & Reclaim your Identity

> Going back to get yourself is what you must do to go forward. Essentially you are resetting your life back on track. Through the process of finding self, self-expression and awakening your identity in Christ.

RESET: Press the Restart Button!

According to Merriam Webster's Dictionary, the word RESET means "to start anew, to resume (something, such as an activity) after interruption". Your life and spiritual walk may have been interrupted but today begins your RESET!

In Chapter 1, you took re-possession of your life back, and in Chapter 2, you retrieved practical and biblical truths to wash away the false doctrines and belief systems. You forgave and released the pain out of your hearts to start anew. In this chapter, we will focus on **resetting who you are. Through the process of finding**

Step 3: Reset & Reclaim your Identity

self, self-expression and awakening your identity in Christ.

Finding Self

Going back to get yourself is what you must do to go forward! **You may even backslide in your faith in this process as you are navigating your way forward. I found this process to be fun and turbulent at the same time. The fun parts are walking through a process of self-discovery and exploration of new opportunities. The turbulence would come into play when challenged with religious views of how it perceived my transformation process.**

Now I'm going to give you a warning upfront. Your friends and family may be shocked by what that might look like for you. It's kind of like having a mid-life crisis whereby you're trying to figure out your identity. In doing so, some have done unusual things for them like shaving off long hair, getting tattoos, clubbing, smoking, and drinking. All sorts of things can happen in this process of finding yourself in an 'identity crisis.' You might want to hold yourself accountable to a trusted friend to ensure that someone can pull your coat tail if need be.

People watching you go through this process may express that you are not growing. They may even question if you are even saved or say things like "You appear to be stuck and deforming." On the contrary, you are re-building

Step 3: Reset & Reclaim your Identity

yourself back, and doing that, you have to go back and get the 'real self' that you were before you were traumatized by a controlling church. That means that you have to remember what you liked, what you disliked, what your opinions are, what styles of fashion you enjoyed wearing and the places that you would enjoy going to.

Another perspective is that you may make healthy changes that could appear to some as drastic; wearing earrings, dying your hair red, wearing pants and makeup, including colors in your wardrobe, or buying whatever you desire regardless of price. You are taking control of the way that you present yourself to the world. Though it may be modest and decent, it still may pose a problem in your network. On the other hand, there will be some that couldn't wait to see this day when you get to be free and not so rigid in your beliefs and your idea of self-expression.

Going over who you were as a person before you were entangled with the church is an excellent start to move forward. This is where you will exercise owning who you are despite people's opinions about how you heal and move on.

Dress Who You Are

There was a time when I was made to think and feel that there was something wrong with me for desiring to dress, what other's would call 'high fashion'. See, I'm from

Step 3: Reset & Reclaim your Identity

London, and you know the UK is known for its fashion. But my pastor then had me looking like an older woman for no reason. My sense of style should have been off-limits for a full-on critique, especially as I dressed modestly and decently. There is no biblical reason why we should not be allowed to wear according to our taste of style and color.

First impressions are indeed lasting impressions. Religious leaders acting as the Fashion Police to the extent that people are in fear of wearing their desired choice is something we need to be careful of practicing. And of course, I am not talking about dressing inappropriately. For example, if you go to an interview, there is an expectation of wearing a shirt and khakis or a suit. The same thing with the church; there is an acceptable standard. I am referring to the extremists who scold individuals for wearing underwear to church. Yes, there is an actual church pastor that has made it a law that the women are not allowed to wear any top and bottom underwear to church. I know this is appalling and is a violation of a basic human right. This leader found a way to use his spiritual authority to stop the members from deciding for themselves how to personally take care of themselves and present their 'Self' to the world. This violation strips their ability to think on a fundamental level and keeps them under the leader's control.

My point is that in this process, you will be testing different ideas and self-expression as a way to form and

Step 3: Reset & Reclaim your Identity

establish your 'self-identity.' Clothing is essential as it is a representation of who you are.

The Cloning Factory

Narcissists purposely clone their members and use clothing to enforce conformity in unison. Now that you have left, you have the opportunity to choose what to wear, what car you'll buy, where you want to live, to go back to work and or school. These are your decisions, just use them wisely, which in itself is a process of trial and error. You'll swing to the left, then to the far right before you work your way into the middle for a happy and well-balanced medium.

Sometimes you'll make the right decisions for your life, and other times you won't. It's just a learning curve to trust your instincts and not to always second guess yourself. You've got to be comfortable and compassionate towards yourself, especially when you make mistakes.

Remember, you are having to challenge the voices of teachings and doctrines that will speak back to you and try to dictate to you what you should be doing with your life according to the narcissistic culture.

You would think that since you left that you could move on quickly. Well, if you think about it, you went through a process of programming. The culture there was to break down your sense of self to build worshipping robots. To do this, the leader manipulated the members

Step 3: Reset & Reclaim your Identity

to compromise their own beliefs and standards of daily operations and then broke into the psyche for a hostile takeover. The commander at the control station is no longer your 'Self' person but the narcissistic leader. And whatever buttons they press, you react like a puppet. Thank goodness you escaped, and you understand that many things you were taught do not carry more weight than the Bible.

Do You Know who You are?

During my journey, there was a time when I was inwardly withdrawn, basically I was depressed. I was despondent and hid from myself, from everybody else and the world. The Holy Spirit was trying to jump-start my identity back in alignment with my DNA.

I want to ask you a question, and I want you to think very deeply about this.

- Do you know who you are?
- Do you know your role on this earth?
- Do you know who you belong to?

It will take some time to figure this out. But these were the three questions I would hear the Holy Spirit ask me over and over again.

Step 3: Reset & Reclaim your Identity

Your Pain Will Forge Your Purpose

The Bible says that our identity is hidden in Christ in God (Colossians 3:3). Nobody around me understood the internal battles I was dealing with, not even myself. I was in so much fear that I would hide the fear that I was experiencing. I would project the image of a strong black woman, a strong mother, a strong leader, and a reliable armor bearer for my narcissistic pastors. But I thank God that He did not give up on me. He created each of us with a specific purpose. In the book of Jeremiah, chapter 29:11 says:

> *"For I know the thoughts that I think toward you, says the Lord, thoughts of peace and not of evil, to give you a future and a hope".*

I had a future, and God wanted me to know that. He has plans for you like He had plans for me. It is not in the mind of God that you should experience pain and trauma and not overcome it.

Romans 8:28 says:

> *"And we know that all things work together for good to those who love God, to those who are called according to His purpose."*

Step 3: Reset & Reclaim your Identity

What you have experienced will be used for good. Depending on where you are on your journey, you may not think it is possible. But I'm here to share with you that God has a plan for your recovery and a soaring comeback! I never knew that I would be able to tell my story without ever being angry. It amazes me how grateful people are when I share my story. They testify how much of their true self, hopes, and dreams came back alive. In my book 'Run for your Life', I wrote about my journey, my testimony of spiritual abuse, and go further into detail with the sting of betrayal in my book 'Uncovering the Betrayal of Spiritual Abuse.'

Who would have known that I would have written five books and more on this one subject? This subject is very dear to the heart of God. Jesus is the Good Shepherd, and He loves His sheep. The Bible says in Matthew 9:36:

"When He saw the multitudes, He was moved with compassion for them, because they were [b]weary and scattered, like sheep having no shepherd."

Jesus was moved by compassion. He saw the state of the lives of His people and He was deeply concerned that the people had no Shepherd. Jesus, being a Shepherd, is concerned when people are not receiving the adequate and proper shepherding by a leader.

In 2016, I had worked my sister's patience to the point she was blunt and in my face about what I needed

Step 3: Reset & Reclaim your Identity

to change. She held me accountable to start listening to preaching on periscope. Within 2 days of listening to Apostle John Eckhardt he said that he would be coming to Boston. Wow look at God, in my neighbourhood. The Boston Reset Conference was hosted by Apostle James Duncan and Prophetess Dawn Wellington, who are now my leaders.

At the conference I received a prophetic word that I was complaining about the hurt and betrayal that I had experienced. The prophet added "but God said, "You keep asking why, why did this happen, but what God does not hear you asking Him is what was the lesson." This word was like thunder, lightning, and a hammer that broke through the darkness and revealed the light. It was like a Saul turn Apostle Paul experience. The moment was incredible. Instantly I felt the pain in my heart melt away. As the prophet continued to speak into my life saying, "God said it was a demonstration for the young priests." This revelation allowed me to understand I was in a class module, and it was to teach students what not to do and to develop an understanding of what to do. At this point, it was five and a half years of me walking in the wilderness.

The Wilderness was a place where I was tired, my mind was scattered, and I had no Shepherd. I had little interest in submitting my life to the Lord Jesus. Now I loved God, but I had unresolved issues towards Him and His people. My heart grew cold, condescending, judgmental, and wayward.

Step 3: Reset & Reclaim your Identity

I made up my own religion. I would say, "I'm not religious; I'm just spiritual." That was a cop-out to build a relationship with God according to His word. I was fed up with living the life where the Bible was used to control me, dominate me, and make me feel bad. So it made sense to live my life on my terms according to the flesh. Which I have found is a pattern with those who have been spiritually abused. Their interest in church weans thin as they see it as a place that destroyed their identity and faith. Notice that my deliverance came when I returned to the church. It may not happen this way for you as God can reach you anywhere! My point is that the Body of Christ is still a place of refuge for those who are wounded by the church.

You Are Fearfully Made by God

To build up your sense of worth and value, you have to get connected to your maker, the one that created you, that is God, your heavenly father. I love what the Psalmist David said in Psalm 139:14,

> *"I will praise You, for **I am fearfully and wonderfully made**; Marvelous are Your works, And that **my soul knows** very well".*

You are fearfully and wonderfully made, not fearful, and made. You are so blessed with what God has created you to be that you say how marvelous are your works. I

Step 3: Reset & Reclaim your Identity

will praise you. How often do you look in the mirror and give yourself praise and thank God for your life, for your looks, for your personality, for your traits, for your gifts? Or do you focus on what you think is broken and unfixable? Do you focus on what others project to be considered as attractive and measure yourself to the standard to which you say, "I do not fit the mold, and therefore I am faulty and have no value." This is where you have to change the program that you have allowed to play over and over again in your mind. David said that my soul knows very well. David was referring to his mind, will, and emotion.

You will have to decide to believe what God's word says about you over what you have heard and what you've trusted.

I want you to get to a place where you receive the truth of this word in your soul. This will take some effort and determination on your part. I want you to find some scriptures and take them as a pill for each day. You can use the same scripture over and over again to eradicate words, and feelings that tear you down. This process will get you to a place where you will declare, as David said, *"My soul knows very well."*

Your soul has memory, and we want it to be made pure. Take on this new memory that you are beautiful, you are attractive, you are handsome, you are awesome, you are a child of God, you are talented, you are a great person and have something to contribute to

Step 3: Reset & Reclaim your Identity

society. Cementing this on the blocks of building identity, self-identity, self-esteem, and self-worth from here, you will build self-confidence.

The Potter & the Clay

In Jeremiah 18:1-6, we see God the Creator whom makes and re-makes His people to improve upon what He created. Lifes twists and turns, ups and downs are what are used to shape us or even to get us into shape. I'm sure you've heard this saying before "That which was meant to destroy you is the very thing that God will use to develop you."

"The word which came to Jeremiah from the Lord, saying, Arise and go down to the potter's house, and there I will cause you to hear My words." 3 Then I went down to the potter's house, and there he was, making something at the [a]wheel. 4 And the vessel that he [b]made of clay was [c]marred in the hand of the potter; so **he made it again into another vessel, as it seemed good to the potter to make.**

5 Then the word of the Lord came to me, saying: 6 "O house of Israel, can I not do with you as this potter?" says the Lord. "Look, as the clay is in the potter's hand, so are you in My hand, O house of Israel!". (Jeremiah 18:1-6).

This is a time to trust that you are in the capable hands of your Maker to form you. It is the year to fulfill the calling and purposes that He had decided before the

Step 3: Reset & Reclaim your Identity

foundations of the world for you to walk in confidently knowing who you are, whose you are, and your role on this earth.

CHAPTER 4

Step 4: Rebuilding You!

> The rebuilding process involves reclaiming your 'Self-Identity'. You are rescuing and delivering your soul from an undesirable state to restore it to a healthy natural state. This involves establishing boundaries and developing your self-esteem, self-respect and self-confidence.

According to Merriam Webster's Dictionary, 'Rebuild' is defined as "to make extensive repairs" *and* "to restore to a previous state". Step 4 is about rebuilding you. You are like a city/temple that has been ruined and looks unrecognizable to its former glory.

When a contractor rebuilds a house, they create new updates, additions to renovate the property. The restoration work takes money, time, and effort. When the house is on the market for sale, the new owners get to enjoy its new improved value. This value causes the new owners to feel esteemed. Because of the new siding, landscape, open-floor plan and additional rooms and or bathrooms to the property, it creates the potential for a positive impact to the value of the other homes in

Step 4: Rebuilding You!

that area. When you are fully restored, you will add to the lives of those in your company. You will operate in a higher version of yourself and cause others to grow also. You are building an upgraded version of you and your life will pave the way for others because you decided to be remodeled and up-leveled!

Professional Boundaries: Develop a Higher Standard, Set & Communicate Your Expectations

According to Merriam Webster's Dictionary, a standard is a flag and or banner. It is also described as: That which is established by authority as a rule for the measure of quantity, extent, value, or quality;

The Bible tells us in Isaiah 59:19 that: *"When the enemy comes in like a flood, The Spirit of the Lord will lift up a standard against him".* What is a standard? The word standard in He brew is translated as flag, banner, boundary and token.

A standard helps you to establish a boundary line, of what is acceptable and unacceptable behavior. It helps to make things clear and put them in a framework as a set of criteria in which to inform, what you would allow, or disallow. If you think about it, the Human Resources personnel's orientation process is to establish the company's policies and procedures, which will govern the new candidate's behavior and attitude. This is a set

Step 4: Rebuilding You!

of guidelines to ensure that they professionally represent the company. The company requires their agreement as they lay down their set of standards. If there is a breach of the agreement, the standards will expose where you did not comply. These standards also support both parties in the process of working together. The question is, what standard have you made clear for others to abide by? What have you told them that you will tolerate or not tolerate? Interestingly, standard is translated as a flag, a banner, something that you would wave in the air. Sometimes in relationships, we see red flags; these are signals waving in front of our faces in mid-air to get our attention. They act as a communication device speaking to us, but many times we have made choices to ignore it.

Merriam Webster's Dictionary offers another definition and states, it is "a structure built for or serving as a base or support".

You see, the purpose of having a standard is not to be defensive, closed off, standoffish, or to walk around with a chip on your shoulder, making people feel that they owe you something. No, the reason is just to serve as support.

Re-Establish Your Boundaries

According to Merriam Webster's Dictionary, the definition of establish is "to institute (something, such as a law) permanently by enactment or agreement, to make firm or stable, to introduce and cause to grow and multiply, to

Step 4: Rebuilding You!

bring into existence." In this chapter, you will learn how to re-establish boundaries to cause you to grow and attract healthy relationships. We will be looking at outdated boundaries to reaffirm and reestablish new ones.

Establishing healthy boundaries changes the way you are received, treated, and speaks loudly about how much you value yourself. When people have suffered from abuse, no matter what type of abuse, it means that their boundaries are violated. Look at it this way, you are like a city, and to keep the city safe, you have to have guards to decipher if and when the enemy is drawing close. Entry points to your city would be the gates to go in and out. You are a Watchman for your life but, if you are not taught the proper expectations and boundaries, you will forfeit your duty to stand guard to protect.

The Bible tells us in Matthew 7:15,

"Beware of false prophets, who come to you in sheep's clothing, but inwardly they are ravenous wolves".

Unfortunately, this is a reality that some run unethical operations under the guise of the gospel. But I'm glad that it is noted in the Bible so that we can keep watch vigilantly.

Further along, this passage states in Matthew 7:16-20,

Step 4: Rebuilding You!

*"**You will know them by their fruits**. Do men gather grapes from thornbushes or figs from thistles? 17 Even so, every good tree bears good fruit, but a bad tree bears bad fruit. 18 A good tree cannot bear bad fruit, nor can a bad tree bear good fruit. 19 Every tree that does not bear good fruit is cut down and thrown into the fire. 20 **Therefore <u>by their fruits, you will know them</u>**."*

This passage explains the relationship between us and knowing people's traits and characteristics. Are you a good judge of character? If all you know is abuse and that's all you have been able to attract in your life, then this becomes a norm. This creates an inability to discern, assess, and to evaluate and to respond to danger i.e. red flags. Observing, inspecting, and even investigating the integrity of fruit is what is lacking. You may look at the appearance and judge that it must be good to partake in and eat.

We know that Eve was deceived and seduced into accepting the cunning words of the snake in the garden. She did not investigate, pry or fact check the devil's words against God's instructions spoken to her and Adam. The reason being is because the devil's strategy was subtle.

The meaning of subtle, according to Merriam Webster's Dictionary, is highly skillful and challenging to understand and perceive. The devil appears to be harmless. He uses his intelligence knowing that **subtlety is a**

Step 4: Rebuilding You!

weapon that could take on the appearance of a thing. Its ability to be camouflaged makes it difficult for the weapon of subtlety to be detected. To be able to discern a fake product, you would have to study the genuine product, and it's most delicate of details so that when an imitation product comes your way, you would know it's true worth and status. Ladies, we love our handbags and shoes and we also know a real one from a fake too. Now it's okay to buy the imitation as long as that's your choice and you are buying it knowing it is an imitation. The tragedy is when you don't know the item is a fake Coach bag and you get ripped off by a fast-talking salesperson.

This happened to me almost 20 years ago. Versace just came on the scene but I hadn't studied it. I did find a beautiful imitation belt for $50gbp and I fell for it because of the price. I knew a designer would cost way more than the average belt but failed to research or look closer at its logo and the quality of the product. That's how I got bamboozled! It only took a few wears before the gold plate wore off. That's when I knew the truth.

My point is this….It is easy to be dazzled and bamboozled by narcissits when you are new in your faith or when you have a desperate need. It is easy under both circumstances because you either don't have enough information to fact check and so you rely on the narcissist to tell you the truth. Or you are mature but are experiencing a crisis, loss, or in need. This causes you to choose to believe in the narcissist as a means to receive your breakthrough.

Step 4: Rebuilding You!

Therefore you forgo every warning as to not jeporadize your opportunity to receive your blessing. Both types of people are not paying close attention to facts, intentions and motives of the narcisisits heart.

The more you study the Bible and spend time with God, the more He will reveal His heart and thoughts. The Bible is our boundary line! It is our fact checker system, and we must study it to be more aware of God's ways. The Bible is data to measure against falsehood, evil, and unrighteousness. The devil plays on our ignorance. The Bible tells us in Hosea 4:6, *"My people are destroyed for lack of knowledge."*

The problem is that narcissits provide a lot of information and teaching and extra classes for it's members to consume their content. This process lulls the people to sleep and prevents them from thinking and researching the Bible for themselves. This is could brainwashing. Unknowingly the people are hypnotized and are desensitized to a desire of seeking God in the Bible, which is their boundary. **Instead they have fallen into the trap of looking to their leader for truth on how to live as a Christian. The leader is now in control and becomes their boundary, a standard to live by.**

It is essential to understand that the weapon of lies, deceit, deception, subtlety, and seduction are used to persuade and manipulate you to make decisions that override your boundaries to benefit the deceiver.

Step 4: Rebuilding You!

Boundaries that Block a Positive Flow

You can be a city left unguarded or a city overly guarded. If over guarded, this could be counterproductive. Your defense mechanisms can be hypersensitive and create an inability to receive love, friendship, and the joys of life through people. **You may find yourself overly compensating for having the vault gates wide open without a detection system that did not protect you from a cultic church.** These defense mechanisms are misplaced and allow for even more rejection as you push people away. Both are harmful and not healthy.

To rectify this, you need to be open to how the Holy Spirit will instruct you to carry yourself. Seek out the Holy Spirit to teach you in the word, how to live according to godly principles and standards that will support you. Know that as you heal, this could change. I remember that during my process, there was a time in my fifth-year marker that God said He was preparing me to submit to authority. At that time, I was non-committal to attending church. I had to brace myself for new relationships that were coming into my life. But because God was leading me I had a sense of security that everything would work out fine, as it was His will.

Saying No

One way of knowing that you have low self-worth is by teaching people that it is okay for them to mistreat you, mishandle and ridicule you. This happens when you don't know how to say "No" and say "Yes" when you really want to say "No". You have to practice speaking up for yourself and learn to stand in your position without wavering, giving a bunch of excuses and avoiding to communicate. Remember your silence can be viewed as agreement, so no, your avoidance doesn't always work. You have to learn how to be assertive. Until you commit to this process, you will realize that little events keep popping up that give you opportunities to be assertive. Go for it! Stand and be courageous to support or defend yourself, no matter who you are dealing with in life.

Spiritual Boundaries

The Bible tells us to give honor to whom honor is and teaches us to show respect for those in godly leadership. When a wolf leadership confronts us, we often feel paralyzed and powerless to speak up. As a body, we do not teach one how to approach leadership about sensitive matters of questionable or inappropriate behavior and who we should go to for clarification and or support.

We have not built language to articulate all protocols that would keep all parties safe in respect of narcissistic, Jezebelic cult leadership. This is partly why it is difficult for anybody to speak up and address behaviours that causes harm and or abuse. So, in other words, because of the spiritual principle of honoring godly leadership,

Step 4: Rebuilding You!

which is set by God, we have to take responsibility as a church to support believers with a system or protocol for when things go terribly wrong. These are the Watchmen duties in the church. But if the Watchman has not been trained with an eye to detect and a nose to sniff out demonic intrusion in the church, then the enemy has the range to run rampant, causing many to be injured in the process.

Walls of a city are in place to defend the city. God promised the children of Israel that He would be their wall of defense. Trust God to protect you! Meanwhile, adopt and increase your prayer life for divine protection to detect strategies to war against the enemy.

Low self-esteem, and a lack of self-love, and self-confidence show the route to why the walls are taken down, in replacement to be accepted and approved by others. When you do this, you trade your soul to another. Remember, the narcissist does not have feelings and is not tied to supporting your emotional needs. Instead, they look for your weakness so that they can use it as leverage to get what they want from you.

As long as you have not taken the necessary steps to work on building your self-esteem and self-confidence, individuals will always attach themselves to you to abuse you, that is whether they are in a church leadership position or not. This could happen on your job; it could be a manager that would use their position of power to intimidate, threaten and dominate you. So, you see this life work on building your self-worth is crucial for you to live the life that God has designed for you.

Sometimes we think that spiritual abuse is exclusive to the church...not at all! Those who abuse power in the church are demonically oppressed and could be positioned anywhere in life: business corporations, politics, education, science, medical, and or entertainment industries. Yes, I agree that the fact that they claim to know God, hear God, and walk with God marks a blow to our hearts. The feelings of betrayal are intensified because of the level of trust we gave the individual or group. Preventing this from happening again, statistics show most people will go back into an oppressive relationship group because of the familiarity. Building up your self-esteem causes you to no longer become used to or familiar with abuse.

Here is a list of signs of low self-worth:

- Afraid to say "No"
- Lack of self-respect
- Avoids conflict and or confrontation
- Not trusting your instincts
- Apologizing without blame
- Abusive critical self-talk
- Afraid to speak up
- Inability to protect vulnerabilities
- Suffers from self-rejection
- Feels unworthy of someone's love and or attention

Step 4: Rebuilding You!

How to Develop Personal boundaries

Your self-esteem was developed in your formative years under the care of parents and caretakers. Traumatic events in life are what typically damages our self-esteem. Your work is to promote self-talk to build a positive self-image which will, in turn, build the foundation of your self-worth. Healing the inner child and the internal bruises on your psyche is how the child will grow into an adult performing at a higher state of being.

As a child, you may not have been taught to develop boundaries other than the usual: "Don't take candy from strangers, don't eat at anybody's house, and no you can't stay over your friend's house". These were sayings that I remember my mom saying to me. But I struggled and developed relationships with people that would use me and take advantage of me. I remember in my early twenties, trying to figure out what was going on with my friendships. I concluded that people were taking my kindness for weakness. This was an aha moment for me. It wasn't that I deserved to be mistreated but it was because the individual knew that they could get away with bullying me. After all, my need was friendship. This led to tolerating disrespect in boyfriend relationships and associations. Despite having figured it out, I found it too taxing to work on my damaged self-esteem, which was already wounded from my childhood. I was parented

Step 4: Rebuilding You!

by a father who was violent, non-affirming, critical, and verbally abusive.

If I had prioritized building my self-esteem, developing a positive self-image, and boosting my self-confidence, I would have been able to protect myself from spiritual leaders that prey on young believers. They target the young, so that they can avoid any form of resistance to their wicked ways.

"Below is a list of expectations of a controlling leader that is considered unreasonable and removes the individual's power of choice and free will.

Examine the list below and determine if there is any resemblance to your own experience:

- Not allowed to go on vacation without approval and in most cases, the approval is not
- Not allowed to take a job or go back to school outside of the church
- Not allowed to become a Godparent to someone who is not in the sect.
- Members' children are not allowed to attend public school but instead are forced to
- participate in the church's school for children.
- Not allowed to have intimate relations with their spouse unless approved.
- Not allowed to decide when to have children as it will interfere with their availability
- to push the church's vision.

Step 4: Rebuilding You!

- Not allowed to have family time until a specified time and day decided by the church.
- Not allowed to spend money on family time and/or entertainment as this money must
- be used for the church.
- Not allowed to wear make-up, trousers, jewelry.
- Not allowed to develop their personal style of dressing even if modest.
- Not allowed to visit other churches.
- Not allowed to miss a church service regardless of mitigating circumstances.
- Not allowed to express your opinion.
- Not allowed to question authority, even if in a humble manner.
- Not allowed to read the Bible without the leader's interpretation.
- Not allowed to be counseled by leadership together as husband and wife, counseled
- separately as per church policy.
- Not allowed to partake in the 9 Gifts of the Holy Spirit.
- Not allowed to leave the church without being released by church leadership.
- Not allowed to wear underwear to church.
- Not allowed to buy premium products.
- Not allowed to move residences either local or out of state.

Step 4: Rebuilding You!

***This list is also available to download at www.rebuildbonus.com

Some of these I have experienced myself and or have been asked to enforce these rules over others. Then there are some that I have heard from others.

I implemented and projected some of these rules onto church members. I did it because I felt I had no choice and feared the repercussions of not following through with the leader's instructions.

Know that when I left this church, I called those that I had hurt in my role as a leader and repented seeking their forgiveness. I pleaded with them and told them that that was not the real me that I had taken on a role and lost all feelings of who I was and allowed myself to become a puppet manipulated by a religious, controlling, and legalistic spirit. (Jenkins. M, 2020 "Run For Your Life Book", p122-126)

Reflection:

1. Write down any thoughts and feelings that come up for you in this list.
2. How best could you respond if you are asked to do something that is not aligned with godly integrity?
3. What biblical references can you identify that would or would not support these expectations?

Step 4: Rebuilding You!

4. Identify who in your life you can seek support to voice your opinion and or expectations?

Reclaim Self

Now that you have have understood the importance of establishing boundaries, you can begin to reclaim your 'Self' by build your self-esteem and confidence level.

Definition of Reclaim:
According to Merriam Webster's Dictionary, reclaim is defined as "to rescue from an undesirable state and or to restore to a previous natural state." **The rebuilding process involves reclaiming your 'Self-Identity'. You are rescuing and delivering your soul from an undesirable state to restore it to a healthy natural state.**

Oftentimes these words self esteem and self-confidence are used interchangeably. I will explain the difference.

Definition of Self-Worth:
According to Merriam Webster's Dictionary, self-worth is defined as "**a sense of one's own value as a human being**".

The question is, do you believe that as a human being that you have value? Before you answer I don't want you to think about your shortcomings or your talents. Your self-worth is not based on how well you perform or what

Step 4: Rebuilding You!

you are not good at. It's a lot simpler than that. You are a human being therefore you are valuable.

The antidote to building self-worth is believing that you deserve to be treated with respect. Self-respect is demonstrated by what you tolerate and what you don't tolerate by the boundaries you set in place.

To address low self-worth, you have to know that you are valuable and are not less valuable than another person and that somebody else is not better than you.

Definition of Self-Respect:
According to Merriam Webster's Dictionary's Dictionary, self-respect is defined as "**proper respect for oneself as a human being**: regard for one's own standing or position".

Definition of Self-Esteem:
According to Merriam Webster's Dictionary, self-esteem is defined as "**confidence and satisfaction in oneself**".

This is a great definition that leads you to ask yourself the question, are you satisfied with who you are as a person, as a human being? Are you happy, do you feel fulfilled, do you feel like you have made accomplishments to be proud of yourself? And the hardest question of them all is do you love yourself? Are you able to accept your flaws, your mistakes, and count all as a learning experience instead of an opportunity to guilt-trip yourself into a negative spiral?

Step 4: Rebuilding You!

The Bible tells us in Romans 3:23-25, *"For all have sinned and fall short of the glory of God, 24 being justified [a]freely by His grace through the redemption that is in Christ Jesus, 25 whom God set forth as a [b]propitiation by His blood, through faith, to demonstrate His righteousness, because in His forbearance God had passed over the sins that were previously committed."*

Note to self, we have all sinned and have fallen short. **Therefore**, you are not to **feel** inferior, feeling less than anybody else. In the eyes of God, we are all sinners. But according to this scripture, the redemptive work of Christ Jesus that He shed His blood for you. He considered you worthy to die a gruesome death that you may be justified and forgiven by His grace. You may not feel that you deserve to be loved. You have to receive it as part of a decision and not based on a feeling. You do this by studying the Bible and believing what God said about you. Anytime the programming of disapproval says "Oh you're not good enough!", you need to shut it down and speak the word of life over yourself.

Religious and Legalistic Doctrines

Religious and legalistic teachings and doctrines work hard to make you feel less than and that is by your works that you are saved, approved, and loved. You may be worn out by trying to prove yourself worthy of attention or

Step 4: Rebuilding You!

exhausted from avoiding disapproval. You may have even left your church or toxic relationships. But still, you are being controlled by internal voices that support inferior programming. You may have also realized that you are enacting a set of behaviors even though you have left the cultic church and are grafted into a new church, led by healthy leadership. This is how you can tell that the healing and deliverance work still has not been completed and that residue is going unchecked. When I see this happening, it breaks my heart because even though the person is free from the abuse, they are still bound, trapped, and unable to experience freedom in Christ to its fullness. The enemy holds them back, and they are unable to trust again and navigate their way into being equipped for their ministry role in the body of Christ.

It is imperative that you seek out support, that you keep on knocking, that you keep on asking until you have found the answer. Then it's your choice to walk the answer. Too many people in the body of Christ are walking around like the living dead. Their emotions are cut off from recognizing that they are not walking in the abundant life. Jesus wants you healed and whole. He is the healer and He will heal you if you press-in like the woman with the issue of blood. You cannot say that you want to be free but then you don't want to be submitted under the leadership, but yet you still want to operate in your spiritual giftings on your own accord. I have seen this many times and have talked about this in more detail

Step 4: Rebuilding You!

in my book *God's Mercy in the wilderness; A Guide to Finding your Calling and Purpose in the Midst of Church Hurt.*

The affirmation that you seek from man, you have to now acknowledge that God is the only one; your heavenly father is the only person that can give you the self-affirmation that you need to keep your self-esteem intact and to build it to be healthy. It is an unhealthy expectation to look for it elsewhere. This is how you give away your self-power and in return, you have left yourself vulnerable to the attacks of all those who do not respect or value you. Walk in confidence not hurt! Be aware of the stories you are telling yourself that you call truths. These stories are not your truth, you can change how you are received and treated in this world, but it starts from within. The question is, how well are you taking care of yourself?

Self Confidence

According to the psychology dictionary, self-confidence is stated as the following:

> *"Our self-assurance in trusting our abilities, capacities, and judgments; the belief that we can meet the demands of a task."*

Having confidence is based on your self-belief on whether or not you can be successful when you endeavor a new role, a new task, and or are on a new journey. For

Step 4: Rebuilding You!

example, you could have a healthy level of self-worth, self-esteem and respect but lack self-confidence in traveling on your own to a foreign country, accepting a promotion, and so on. It helps that your self-esteem is healthy because it would direct you to look for help to boost your self-confidence. For example, you may look for a course to teach you the know-how to negotiate a promotion. Such courses may cover self-limiting beliefs that block your confidence and the mastery of negotiation tips and skills. To be confident, you have to be in control of self-talk. If you have an inner conflict at church, your self-talk will encourage you to speak up and be heard. You have something of value to bring to the table, instead of being afraid to speak, in fear of the repercussions of rejection and disapproval that may occur as a result of speaking up. Now, it might happen that you will experience what you feared. However, a healthy state of mind and self-respect would move forward with an understanding that there could be a disagreement but it would not imply that they are a bad person or not good enough.

It is now high time for you to walk in your power in your greatness and with Godly authority. You are establishing your power and tapping into your spiritual power through prayer, reading of the word, and fasting. This is where John talks about the importance of abiding in God.

Step 4: Rebuilding You!

John 15:4-5 says,

"Abide in Me, and I in you. As the branch cannot bear fruit of itself, unless it abides in the vine, neither can you, unless you abide in Me. I am the vine, you are the branches. He who abides in Me, and I in him, bears much fruit; for without Me you can do nothing".

In this season no longer will you walk in insecurities, walking with your head down, afraid to meet new people, afraid to say yes to your dreams, afraid to start looking for a church family to fellowship with.

Psalm 3:3: says, *"But You, O Lord, are a shield for me, My glory and the One who lifts up my head".*

God is your Shield. He will protect you because you have decided to abide, to rest, and to live in him. 1 John 4:4 says,

"He who is in you is greater than he who is in the world. The Greater One Is inside of you so you no longer have to be afraid you are not alone anymore."

Hebrews 13:5 says, *"Let your conduct be without covetousness; be content with such things as you have. For He, Himself has said, "I will never leave you nor forsake you."*

Step 4: Rebuilding You!

No more do you have to covet, be jealous, compare yourself to people's gifts, talents, and feel inadequate, or feel forgotten just because you see somebody else achieve their goals. You must rest in God and be content, knowing that God has promised that He will never leave you or abandon you.

James 1:8 says, *"A double-minded man, is unstable in all his ways."*

Walking in your godly authority causes you not to allow thoughts of doubt and insecure patterns of behavior and reasoning that cause you to mistrust yourself and your decision-making skills. You understand that you are establishing and rebuilding walls in your life. Appreciate and love what God is doing in your life. The work is not yet finished but enjoy the process. This is the time of the reset. Will you have everything in place to restart your life again, recovering everything that the enemy tried to steal from you?

According to the Bible, when a thief is caught, *"He must **restore sevenfold**; He may have to give up all the substance of his house"*. (Proverbs 6:31)

I want you to declare and know in your heart, that this is your recovery, restoration and reset season. Now that you have healed from past issues, it is time to remove the limiting beliefs that prevent you from soaring. This is where we strategize together to walk you through advancing in your Kingdom Assignment.

CHAPTER 5

STEP 5: Re-Establishing your New Life

> **This is the season to build a stable and permanent way of life. In other words you will establish life values, family culture and develop a lifestyle that is restorative and productive.**

Your understanding of the past has been refreshed and you can move forward to now re-establish your new life in Christ! It is time to turn your firm beliefs into a stable way of living. I am so excited for you! These foundational bricks need to be re-laid and built back up again to settle and establish your life to where you can be permanently independent of the church and live a successful life without the need to go back to them. This next stage takes time, commitment, and unity within oneself and or the family.

According to Merriam Webster's Dictionary, **establish** is defined as "To institute (something, such as a law)

STEP 5: Re-Establishing your New Life

permanently by enactment or agreement, to make firm or stable, to introduce and cause to grow and multiply". Establishing your life will cause you to be solid and not flaky. You will grow and produce a life that has deep roots in the fabric of your community, city, children's school, non-profit boards and so on.

Putting Back the Pieces of Your Life Together

When a storm comes to town and wrecks buildings, homes, schools, and so on, it also does way more damage than the eyes can see. Devastating events are overcome by the process of time. It's never an overnight process to re-establish and re-build the city and its community. This situation needs all hands on deck! From those who have time on their hands and can volunteer their time and efforts, those with money and influence, those who are resourceful, and skilled in specialized areas and those who are connected. Help is needed and help is welcomed.

The difference between community storms and personal storms is that you have to be even more receptive to receive help when everybody else is not affected. You may have to give an account of your experience to get the empathy and support needed. For example, if you have not worked in years, it may be a challenge to explain what you have been doing in the meantime, or why your children's educational level is below the city and state

STEP 5: Re-Establishing your New Life

standards, due to poor teaching at the church school or lack of respect for school education as the church was the number one priority. This is a humbling experience for sure but take courage that the house, is undergoing a stripping to be built back up with huge improvements.

Socially it could be a lonely time if all of your friends and family attend the church that you left. Being excommunicated by the church and its members happens very often. In this case, it is the best way to move forward and to establish new relationships, new job, new home, etc.

You may have had to relocate to another area living with friends, relatives, and or seeking refuge in temporary housing. There are varying degrees of the impact of spiritual abuse and I have heard, seen, and have experienced some crazy things. Like credit cards and personal loans and mortgages taken out on behalf of the church and no payments made, destroying credit capabilities. Some have been denied approval from their pastor to go back to school for an education, to work, or to have friends. Some were forced to live with their pastors or in homes run by the church. Some gave up their children to be raised elsewhere to work for the church or attend the church's boarding school. And some may have been involved in criminal activities under the church's instruction and face issues of criminalization and rehabilitation back into the community. None of this mattered. Of course, it was spiritualized to downplay the lack of integrity of the leadership. Now that you have left, it has become a

STEP 5: Re-Establishing your New Life

rude awakening on how much all of these things matter when it comes to being established in society and living independently from the cultic church.

Depending on where you are, you may need to contact your local Social Services Department, to get back on your feet for housing, food, clothing, job, and career services. Personal counseling and or family counseling may also be needed to restore the family's needs, structure, ties, and function. It is really sad to see when children are involved, how angry they feel that their parents were emotionally absent, showed little affection and or concern, or an ability to protect them. All of this in the name of serving God, though in actuality it is idolizing man as a man-pleaser.

This is why it is crucial to take time in your recovery process to rebuild the foundations of your family. According to Maslow's Hierarchy of Needs, your basic needs are housing, love, security, and warmth. This is where your focus should be. If you decide to attend a church, then that's great. What I found out is that as I started to attend local churches, my usual disposition as a servant leader is to get stuck in and help where I can. I felt very guilty that I was not in a church. As time went on, I felt a sigh of relief as I questioned my heart's motive for going to church. **I permitted myself not to draft myself into church leadership positions. Once I did this, I understood that I was running on autopilot and had not yet**

STEP 5: Re-Establishing your New Life

learned the importance of adjusting to civilian life so to speak.

You see, my first response was what I was used to doing. It didn't matter whether or not I wanted to do it. I was trained to always be serve and help others. Walking in that freedom of choice was liberating for me and it allowed us as a family to focus on building our relationships with our children and even talking about the past and laughing about it. We did things like go on vacations every year internationally and nationally. We celebrated the holidays with friends and family. We had fun. We went to several of the Six Flag Parks. We had fun on Sundays and regularly ate out at restaurants as a family of seven. As a couple, we dated every Friday and frequently met ate lunch together during work lunch breaks. Every Wednesday was movie night as a family and we made a point to eat and drink there. We talked about God sometimes and rarely prayed as a family. We did get blessed and worked for great companies doing what we enjoyed and received multiple promotions. By the second year, we bought our first house and later an additional 4-unit building. We also focused on the children's education and got them up to par and then above their peer level.

A key to restoring relationships is to repent for your absence in their life, and anything else that would have brought them pain. Actively listen when they talk about how your behavior hurt their feelings and do not try to justify your behavior. Admit your wrongs and apologize.

STEP 5: Re-Establishing your New Life

The Purposely Driven Life

We had intentionally constructed a vision for the family and pursued to fulfil it. We wanted to ensure that the church would not be able to take credit for any mishap in our lives as it was common practice for them to project word curses on those that left the church which would keep others from leaving. We knew that they expected us to be divorced, poor, and unproductive in life and ministry. We were out to prove them wrong!

I want you to be honest with yourself and reflect on what is driving your decisions concerning rebuilding, your life. What are you building? And how long will it take you to build?

It takes great courage to move on and it takes even greater courage to build, especially when you are starting from scratch. I want you to be encouraged. There is an excitement that comes with the unknown of what will our lives look like in one, five and ten years from now. Feed on the hope of new beginnings. You have nothing to lose but everything to gain.

To build, you must have **a vision** and gain the support of others to come and build with you.

Proverbs 29:18 says, "***Where there is no vision, the people perish***". (KJV)

Keep your vision for yourself and or family alive by talking and planning for it. Find like-minded people who

STEP 5: Re-Establishing your New Life

have similar visions and let your passion grow hot and not cold. I was determined to re-establish and rebuild. Thought processes and habits need to be challenged. It is not easy to change or to maintain motivation. However, **having a clear vision of your future and the goals that you want to meet must be written, spoken, and believed in before you can conceive the new.**

Abram in the Bible was challenged to relocate away from his family in a new country to start a new. **Abram had to establish and rebuild a new foundation for his family, according to the new pattern God was giving him (Genesis 12). The Bible credits him for having faith in God in uncertain times.**

Romans 4:3 *"Abraham believed God, and it was accounted to him for righteousness."*

I want you to dig deep and seek God for his vision for your life....Trust me He has one! Go over the reflective questions below and record your answers in a journal. You can do this on your own or as a couple and share your answers. Please note that your goals may overlap and then there may be some goals that are individualistic and need the support and or agreement of the spouse.

I stayed in the re-establishing and rebuilding stage of my life for a whole five years before the wind of God blew me in a different direction. There is no telling how long it can take you. Just be excited that you have been delivered

STEP 5: Re-Establishing your New Life

from bondage to create a life that you can be proud of. Negative feelings may crop up from time to time. Stay focused. You have grown and you are becoming better. Leave bitterness alone. Don't give it room to seep into your foundation. No complaining or griping, just releasing and keeping a tenacious attitude, to do your best to obtain the prize of building a glorious life for you and your family.

More Reflective Questions:

1. How would you assess your level of happiness about your life?
2. What does establishing and stabilizing your life look like?
3. What issues need to be immediately fixed?
4. What issues must be fixed but you don't know how to resolve it?
5. Who are the people you think can help? Write down their names or roles.

CHAPTER 6

Step 6: REVIVE – Re-Awakening the Spiritual Giant Within

> Step 6, is where God begins to revive and re-awaken you to His presence and His assignment for your life. People and circumstances will be used to to both awaken and support you to find your way back to the Father.

Five years in and I started to get bored. Something was terribly missing. God was missing! God began to draw me back to Him. On the surface, everything was great. I was feeling accomplished as a family. We were established, but something was missing in what we had built. God was speaking that He wanted to be a part of the rest of the house as we built the foundation of our new life.

This step is where God begins to revive and re-awaken you to His presence and His assignment for your life. The void in my heart was difficult to describe at the time. I

Step 6: REVIVE – Re-Awakening the Spiritual Giant Within

remember saying "If I had a heavy crusted cherry pie, it would solve this whole in my heart". I ate the cake, had my favorite food, but still, I kept telling my husband, that nothing I did resolved what was going on inside me. I was baffled as emotionally eating normally solved my problems at least for a moment. It was months later, as God's plans for me became apparent, that it was my spirit that He was tugging on. I had not exercised that part of me for years. I only prayed or read my Bible occasionally.

According to Merriam Webster's Dictionary, **"to revive means to come to your senses, to come back around again, become active or flourish again".** I had stopped breathing in the breath of God that would fuel a spiritual life with God through prayer and His word. And my spirit, soul, and body were regaining back its consciousness of who God is. Mind you, for mostly five years, I had refused personal ministry from anybody. I just did not want anyone to speak into my life. God had to speak to me directly and so He did. The void did not go away until I made a conscious decision to surrender my life and re-dedicate my life back to Christ Jesus.

I'm so glad that the Bible tells us in Jeremiah 3:14-19,

"Return, O backsliding children," says the Lord; **"for I am married to you.** I will take you, one from a city and two from a family, and **I will bring you to Zion.** 15 And **I will give you shepherds according to My heart**, who will feed you with knowledge and understanding."

Step 6: REVIVE – Re-Awakening the Spiritual Giant Within

God is married to the backslider and He promises to bring us back to the place of worship, Zion, and there He promises to give us shepherds that have His heart. They are not manipulators. They are not serving to control, but they are in a position to feed the sheep to be matured, not according to a list of rules and obligations but in Christ.

There is no one right way to recover from this experience. You have to trust the process that you are walking out. It is like being a baby all over again; you're learning to pray, you're learning to feed yourself the Bible, you're learning to hear the voice of God to direct and lead you. It may feel uncomfortable at times because you had been accustomed to people telling you what to do. Just like those who are in prison. When they come out of prison, they are faced with a lot of decisions and responsibilities. Some go back into jail because they are overwhelmed and anxious that they might make a wrong decision and fail. Self-sabotage is a trap that the enemy lays down in hopes to trip you up so you won't bother to do the work to get back on your two feet again.

I think about the prodigal son and Saul, who later was revived and reawakened to become Apostle Paul. Both experienced deliverance from the life they chose. They were rescued and aligned with their true purpose in life.

Prayer Point: Right now, I want you to pray over yourself, decreeing and declaring that God will illuminate your spirit to seek Him out high and low; that your

Step 6: REVIVE – Re-Awakening the Spiritual Giant Within

eyes being enlightened will come to know and walk in the plans God has for your higher calling.

> Ephesians 1:17-19 says,"That the God of our Lord Jesus Christ, the Father of glory, may **give to you the spirit of wisdom and revelation in the knowledge of Him**, 18 the **eyes** of your [a]**understanding being enlightened**; that **you may know what is the hope of His calling**, what are the riches of the glory of His inheritance in the saints, 19 and what is the exceeding greatness of His power toward us who believe, according to the working of His mighty power".

Prayer Point: Pray asking for every evil veil to be removed and every scale of darkness to fall from your eyes that you will not be like the blind guides that lead the blind into a ditch but you will be instructed by God's eyes.

> Acts 9:18 "Immediately there fell from his eyes something like scales, and he received his sight at once; and he arose and was baptized".

Prayer Point: Pray asking that the Holy Spirit will guide you with God's eye to walk in His ways.

> Psalms 32:8 "I will instruct you and teach you in the way you should go; I will guide you with My eye".

Step 6: REVIVE – Re-Awakening the Spiritual Giant Within

Facing challenges

One thing that I am passionate about highlighting as an issue is that...People who have experienced spiritual abuse tend to jeopardize their calling by disowning God and actively fellowshipping in church. I know because this is exactly what I did. There was a time when I was even challenged to believe that there was a God! This was the depth of the effects of the traumatic experience.

I believe if you have a calling and, more specifically, if you are called to be a five-fold minister, you must be equipped. The equipping process occurs during a process of serving and being faithful with another man's vision and submitting to godly authority. When you are not healed then this is the process that you run from for fear of being hurt again. Even worse, if and when your spiritual gifts are activated, e.g. gift of prophecy, healing, and so on, because you can feel the stirring of the gifting inside and you can be compelled to move forward without seeking covering from an established ministry. Some look for networks to join as a way of being connected but remain invisible and unaccountable. Others attach themselves to ministries that are widely known but are not able to provide the levels of intimacy that are needed to work on character flaws, maturation of the gift, and covering for the vision. I'm always leery of these situations, and so that's why I am bringing it to your notice

Step 6: REVIVE – Re-Awakening the Spiritual Giant Within

so that we can limit unnecessary damage in the body of Christ.

Please note that hurting people hurt people. Healed people heal people. It was Maya Angelou who said "When we know better, we do better. I go into much more detail in my book titled *God's Mercy in the Wilderness: A Guide to Finding Your Calling & Purpose in the Midst of Church Hurt*. The reason why this is so close to my heart is that this was almost me.

I almost was about to find myself in a situation where I would operate in my prophetic gifts without accountability and that is because I had an issue trusting leadership. It was evident that I still was not healed because I didn't think that my not trusting leadership was an issue. Thankfully God intervened and put it in order. If not, I would have been a hypocrite and fell into the same pit that traps many blind leaders today.

So I'm a big advocate of REVIVING Your Life, including your Spiritual LIFE! You got wounded inside the church. Yes, me too! But Don't Run from God, run from the abuser by all means. YES! Many opt-out and opt-in on false doctrines and spiritualism and all kinds of rituals of the occult, which only opens up doors of spiritual attacks. Check your motives when you opt-in and out of belief systems to ensure that you are not being misled.

Step 6: REVIVE – Re-Awakening the Spiritual Giant Within

Finding a Church

I want you to be in prayer and ask God to find you a church home. There are plenty of great Bible-based churches around. And if you are already in a church, and you know that you know that's where you are supposed to be but!... You are holding back and doing everything to be invisible. I want you to go in prayer and fast and ask God to help you to move forward. I would attend a weekly prayer call and for years I would hide and come on the call late, deliberately so that I would not be called on to participate by praying as it was their custom. One day the Holy Ghost checked me and told me I was playing games...He explained that I was selfishly taking the goodies i.e. asking for prayer, receiving impartations but refused to give anything back in return. I was focused on me and my needs and was happy with this disposition until He brought it to my attention at this stage. There is a law called the Law of Reciprocity; you reap what you sow. Always taking and not giving is not a principle that activates blessings. My point is, come out of hiding and get plugged in and don't let the enemy torment you with fears and anxieties that what happened in your previous church may happen again. If it does, you know that you can seek help, communicate your expectations, and decide to sever the relationship. You have options and tools. Before you did not know this. Besides you can, according to Matthew 18:15-17, ask to meet with a

Step 6: REVIVE – Re-Awakening the Spiritual Giant Within

witness to resolve any ought or offense...That's the Bible; that's the least you should do if some red flags or offenses that need to be resolved. In resolving the matter, you may even learn that there was no harm intended, it was all a miscommunication and nothing more. Use the tools that I have shared, and you will be okay. If you require more in-depth support, you can always arrange for sessions with me through my coaching services.

Awakening Your Spiritual Giant Within

Okay, so you have prayed and decreed God's alignment over your life, and you have permitted Him to illuminate you in your spirit, causing you to arise as the Giant you are! We talked about finding a church and recognizing that you need the environment that will support your flourishing. You are like a plant that has been watered from a season of being unwatered, dried and brittle and were about to break off. But God came in and held you together with His restorative properties in His breath, word, and church.

You may even feel an unction to pray, fast, study the Bible, and so on.

To make it easier, let's work with a framework to help you stay focused on activating your spiritual walk.

1. **Pray** and surrender all, giving God **permission** to lead you.

Step 6: REVIVE – Re-Awakening the Spiritual Giant Within

Romans 8:14 "For as many as are **led by the Spirit of God**, these are sons of God."

2. **Prophesy** over your life, overturning every season of barrenness to a season of total restoration and **prosperity** even as your **soul prosper**s.

   *Ezekiel 34:4-7 "He said to me, **"Prophesy to these bones**, and **say** to them, 'O dry bones, hear the word of the Lord**! 5 Thus says the Lord God to these bones: "Surely I will cause **breath to enter into you, and you shall live**. 6 I will put sinews on you and bring flesh upon you, cover you with skin, and put breath in you; and you shall live. Then you shall know that I am the Lord." 7 So **I prophesied as I was commanded**; and as I prophesied, there was a **noise**, and **suddenly** a rattling; and the bones **came together**, bone to bone".*

3. **Partnership** - Notice that Ezekiel was commanded to prophesy, to speak to the situation to activate the change for a revival. Breath came to the body and brought life to a dead thing. It is only partnering with God that your spiritual giant can be unleashed. When you believe in the power of God's words, you will see that suddenly you are making noise! Ha-ha, the Lion is awake! Praise God! Your family will hear you praying; your friends will

listen to you speaking differently, you move and sound like the Man or Woman of God that you were always meant to be. Now that does not mean that you fit a mold, but you fit the impression that God as the Potter created you to be.

4. **Promises** - Search for the promises of God and pray and sing them to God, write them down, create affirmations out of them. Decree and declare the promises of God over yourself and situations.

5. **Petition** - Make your requests known to God. Do not fret, do not give up, nor be discouraged. Press into the Holy Ghost for what you need to change.

6. **People** - You are in transition and just like Saul, who was uncertain if he would be able to see again, he had to trust the process. God sent persons such as Ananias and the disciples to guide Saul to receive the care and restoration he needed. Pray for God to send you godly mentors that will lay hands and impart a greater measure of the anointing, grace, and spirit of God on you. That spiritual gifts will be imparted and activated to empower you. You will be mentored/fathered to grow in the things of God like Samuel under Eli, Elisha under Elijah, and Timothy under Paul's tutelage. We see from the account below, that Saul was ministered

Step 6: REVIVE – Re-Awakening the Spiritual Giant Within

to physically, emotionally, and spiritually. This strengthened Saul to the extent that he decided to go all-in, repent, and get baptized. **He was not hiding anymore; he made a public declaration that he is revived in Christ and delivered from religion. He had been revived from walking as a spiritually dead person to now being made alive in Christ.** As you submit to this process of being revived and called out to be the powerhouse you are for Christ, you will be positioned to make a public display of what God has done in you and through you. You may find yourself being re-dedicated, licensed, ordained for God's use. Notice that when Jesus was baptized, it involved a team of people; John the Baptist, the crowd as witnesses, the Holy Spirit as a dove and the voice of Father God (Luke 3:21-22). Team ministry causes personalities to learn how to submit to one another under guidance.

Acts 9:17-19

"And Ananias went his way and entered the house; and laying his hands on him he said,"Brother Saul, the Lord Jesus, who appeared to you on the road as you came, has sent me that you may receive your sight and be filled with the Holy Spirit." 18 Immediately there fell from his eyes something like scales, and he

received his sight at once; and he arose and was baptized. 19 So when he had received food, he was strengthened. Then Saul spent some days with the disciples at Damascus"

7. **Pursue Purpose** - While you are pursuing your purpose, you will find that some things will begin to click while others will challenge you. **My word of caution here is not to allow your past hurts of residue to cause you to sabotage the help that God sends you.** You will be surely tested at this junction which is why you must hold firm on to God's vision and promises for your life. The enemy would love to deceive you from exercising your authority over him, especially in unison with the body of Christ. In this phase of restoration, you are a threat to him as you have awakened the call on your life. Apostle Paul went on to become a spiritual giant, writing two-thirds of the New Testament Bible. My prayer for you is that you will not faint while doing good.

Galatians 6:9 *"And let us not grow weary while doing good, for in due season we shall reap if we do not lose heart."*

***Awakening Your Spiritual Giant is also available to download at www.rebuildbonus. com

CHAPTER 7

Recover - Making a Full Recovery

> We are at our best when we are feeling good about who we are and are walking in our calling and purpose. This step will support you to pursue your purpose, set goals, plan your comeback, and fight for your total recovery.

According to Merriam Webster's Dictionary, it defines 'recover' as "to become healthy and strong again after illness or weakness; heal, improve, and make stronger". It also defines 'recovery' as the process of combating a disorder (such as alcoholism) or a real or perceived problem".

Walking in this step is exciting as new health brings about your total transformation from being in a state of spiritual deprivation and abuse, ill-health and low self-esteem. As you have been walking out this process of combating the trauma of spiritual abuse, your recovery is improving. As you continue, your vitals will show optimum health and you will feel and be strong. Life will take on a new course and meaning for you.

Pursuing Purpose

Most people understand that they are created for a specific purpose. Some were able to discover and identify their purpose and calling early in life. While others are still searching. I want you to ponder on the following questions without any pre-judgment of whether you have the money, skill, or know-how.

- What have you always wanted to do?
- What are some of your aspirations?
- What do you envision for the future for you and your family?
- Do you have a plan and if so, are you able to move forward confidently?
- What inspires, angers, and/or moves you?

Your answers are indicators that can lead you into your passion and your purpose on the road to recovery. Walking in your purpose will cause you to feel rejuvenated. When you find that place where everything clicks together, soul, body, and spirit, you will feel alive again; demonstrating a full recovery in spiritual health.

From my own experience, when I left the cultic church 10 years ago, I found freedom in learning who I was again. That meant my interests in hairdressing, fashion, real estate, being a trainer and speaker all started to bubble to the surface of my heart and mind. It was if the zombie mold was cracking and I became alive again. I was awakened to my gifts and hidden desires to become significant and wanted to make an impact. I became hungry for knowledge to develop my core gifts and purpose in life. In this process, I learned what skills I enjoyed using, which was teaching, training, and speaking. Interests in fashion/make up would consistently come up on career assessments. I reinvented myself and hosted a radio segment named Urban Etiquette for almost 3 years. I taught myself the skills I needed to create and deliver curriculums for career and employment training for high school and for a career readiness program where I worked for 5 years before becoming a Pastor, Real Estate Investor, and Life & Book Coach.

As children, we are unafraid to express what we want to become when we grow up. As we get older, we learn by the responses of our parents, elders, teachers, church leaders, and society what is acceptable and approved ideals for us to become. We lose our faith and belief in ourselves to soar as we face rejection. To this end, I want you to understand that you must permit yourself to dream again. Just like we tell a 3-year-old child...I want to tell you, that you can be anything that you desire to be. I believe that deep down you know exactly what it is you want to do and envision yourself becoming. It is a matter of you giving voice, commitment, energy, and effort to it. The discovery of your purpose will cause you to only end up saying "This was with me all along", "I always enjoyed doing this role or act but I never knew that it was a real thing to apply myself to sharpen". I promise you...Your purpose is inside of you. You are so close to it that you cannot even see it, but most do and I pray you will too! Ask your friends and family for feedback on what your strengths are. Pay attention to the answers that they give you and test it out. Look for mentors and coaches to help you further develop your gifts and talents to monetize. Construct a road map and go after it...pursue your purpose and don't hold back for anybody!

Bounce Back!

Yes, it is most certainly possible to bounce back and to recover all that you lost. The hardest thing to recover is time. You may feel guilty for living in a prisoned church culture and giving your best youthful years to it. Feelings of guilt and shame are what you need to release back to God. Know that He can reposition you so that it would be like you lost no time at all.

Direction

Pursuing your destiny is so much more enriching if you can receive prophetic ministry from ministries that are proven and tried. It was the prophetic ministry that would provide answers to my deepest fears, concerns, and heart issues. God has a way of using people to speak to me to know His will concerning my life. These plans gave me direction.

Proverbs 19:21 *"There are many plans in a man's heart, Nevertheless the Lord's counsel—that will stand."*

When I work with my clients, I love to start by doing a vision board workshop as a live or virtual event. Habakkuk 2:2, *"Write the vision and make it plain on tablets."* The testimonials that I have received say that these events are "lifechanging and empowering". Constructing a vision with God is fun and enlightening.

Proverbs says 29:18 says, (KJV) *"Where there is **no vision**, the people perish: but he that keepeth the law, happy is he".*

Proverbs 29:18 says, *Where there is **no revelation**, the **people cast off restraint**; But happy is he who keeps the law.*

I have placed two translations for Proverbs 29:18. The reason for this is to highlight that vision is insight and revealed knowledge, and hearing what God has for you can bring healing, restoration to lost dreams, breakthroughs, limits broken, and more. I also like the aspect where it says that without this insight *"the people cast off restraint"*. In other words, we live an aimless life without any standards or goals and acccountability. This invites a mundane life when you are created for more. When you develop aspirations to be a business owner, educator, public figure, and so on you, will automatically set standards for your life. You will map out short and long-term goals to accomplish them. You will do everything to elevate and become more to operate at a higher version of yourself.

Spiritual Goals

I want to encourage you to partner up with God by spending more time getting to know Him as a person, not a book with inactive words but a book that is alive. Allow the Holy Spirit to teach you how to grow in Christ. You can set goals to read the Bible for a year, study particular topics and goals to be disciplined and equipped. You may meet these goals in various ways from personal bible study, attending a church, receiving pastoral counseling, mentoring, small Bible study groups, online teaching ministries, and so on.

> Philippians 1:6 says: *"For I am confident of this very thing, that He who began a good work in you will perfect it until the day of Christ Jesus".*

Recovery Affirmations

To find success in any goal, two things are vitally important; visualizations and affirmations. We are accustomed to speaking and claiming our cars, houses, jobs, etc.; we can do the same for our emotional and spiritual health. "**I**

believe that the restoration of your spiritual health is self-care".

Restoring and maintaining your happiness takes effort. When a person is suffering an illness, part of their medical care plan includes the recovery process to heal and fully to function as before the illness, to maintain employment and other life roles. The patient is prescribed medication to be taken consistently, exercises to develop flexibility, muscle tone, and strength, if not the body can deteriorate. If the patient lacks motivation and enthusiasm to follow through with the medical recommendations, then the patient is countering the potential for optimum health benefits. To get the best out of your recovery season it takes commitment, discipline, and vision.

According to Merriam Webster's Dictionary, it gives these **3 definitions for the word 'Recover'; reclaim, bounce back and restore.**

1. To get again in one's possession (reclaim)
   Declare: I have reclaimed my life back!
2. To regain a former or normal state (bounce back, revive)
   Declare: I am revived again and I have bounced back
3. To become healthy and strong again after illness or weakness (heal, improve and make stronger)
   Declare: I am totally healed, totally restored, and have made a powerful comeback!

To maintain your sense of power, use these self-affirmations, and create new ones to direct your thoughts to create a powerful state of mind as opposed to a victim or defeatist mindset. You are powerful and you have to walk in that knowledge.

Be Ready to Fight for Your Success

Be ready to fight for your success! Remember now that the enemy is your adversary and will not like that you have found a way to move forward. You are experiencing freedom in your thoughts, emotions, and in your ability to make decisions because you have learned to even say "No". To keep building your momentum, you will need to identify distractions and self-sabotaging behaviors. This is important because the enemy will seek an advantage to pull you away from being fully restored as a person. I just don't want you healed from the traumatic experiences of spiritual abuse but I want you to be totally restored in every area of your life.

Naaman in the Bible was suffering from leprosy; a skin condition that affected him mentally and emotionally. Despite being famous and a captain for the king, you can imagine how stigmatized he felt and how desperate he wanted to be healed. He was directed to seek a prophet named Elisha for his healing. He was instructed to bathe seven times in the river Jordan which he felt was filthy and beneath him. But actually it was the very thing

Recover - Making a Full Recovery

that activated his healing. He came out of the river with new baby-like skin. What I find interesting is that the King James Version Bible in 2 Kings 5:3, says that God would '**_Recover_**' while other translations use the words cure, healed, and cleaned.

2 Kings 5:3 *"Recover him of his leprosy"* KJV

Recovery from spiritual abuse encompasses the whole man. You are being cured, healed, cleansed, restored, recovered, and are bouncing back to a new normal that was better than your previous state. God recovered Naaman from a disease that brought shame, internalized pain from rejection, and self-hate. God healed his skin and in addition, he became saved and vowed to worship the God of Israel. You see the recovery process is the full package; soul, body, and spirit. The number seven is the number of completion and perfection. Naaman's healing was complete and perfected when his spiritual life came together and he vowed to serve and worship God. Isn't that what the children of Israel did? Remember they left Egypt where they were under the hand of a taskmaster and were set free to journey to a place where they could worship God. This brings us to the point that you were created and placed on this earth to give God glory! WOW! Your journey of deliverance will perfect your relationship back to the Father for a full recovery! Glory!

Your identity will be restored, and your presentation will command honor and respect for the shame that you endured. You have become whole and living a life on purpose to make a significant impact in this world.

Jesus taught in Matthew 5:13-16, *13 "**You are the salt of the earth**; but if the salt loses its flavor, how shall it be seasoned? It is then good for nothing but to be thrown out and trampled underfoot by men.*

You are salt and carry God's DNA flavor. Wherever you go you have an ability to sprinkle season to make an impact for change and improvement.

*14 **You are the light of the world**. A city that is set on a hill cannot be hidden. 15 Nor do they light a lamp and put it under a basket, but on a lampstand, and it gives light to all who are in the house. 16 **Let your light so shine before men, that they may see your good works and glorify your Father** in heaven".*

Don't try to hide anymore; that season is over. God wants you seen so that His glory on your life will bring Him glory. Let your works shine brightly, not dimly. When we started, we acknowledged the pain of suffering in the hands of others you looked up to. Now the pain has gone and you are happy and inspired. Remain ignited and walk in the illumination of God's light. Shine authentically!

Conclusion

As I pointed out earlier, in the Merriam Webster's Dictionary, recovery encompasses the concepts of repossessing what was lost, gaining back your identity and faith in God, and creating a comeback! This is the recovery process and I hope this book has been informative and enlightening for you to keep going without ever looking back!

I pray that you gain the courage to talk about your testimony and share with others what you have learned. I pray that this empowers you to gain some good out of it to help others. This is how we are being used to stop this plague in the church.

My prayer for you is Total Restoration. I want to hear all about your breakthrough aha's and your incredible new life! Contact me and let me know. I want to hear all about it. Also, don't forget **I have the seven steps to this framework mapped out for you to go over and download as a gift for purchasing this book at www.rebuildbonus.com**

Other Contributions

This next section of other voices I added to help support your understanding that you are not alone in this situation. Many have gone on to live full lives by restoring their self-image and zest for life. There is also no right and wrong way to be restored. We can only trust the leading of the Holy Spirit to bring us out. **I hope that the seven steps have been informative for you to use as a guideline to assess, evaluate, and plan your best life!**

Enjoy reading the following chapter written by Co-Author Myria D. Thompson and the written interviews of Prophetess Dawn Akita Wellington and DeShonda Jennings. Feel free to reach out to them.

CHAPTER 8

I am More than a Conqueror

BIO

My name is Myria D. Thompson and I am originally from Oklahoma but currently live in central Virginia with my husband and son. My educational background consists of a BS in Psychology, M.Ed. in Education, and an Educational Specialist degree in Curriculum and Instruction. I have taught in the public-school sector over the last 14 years in special education. My mission in life is to see people healed, delivered, and set free in all areas of their lives.

I am More than a Conqueror

Name: Myria D. Thompson
Email: myriathompson@yahoo.com

Sitting at my desk, attempting to complete a task, I began to hear a phrase over and over, and that was...You are "more than a conqueror." The more that I continued to hear the phrase, I realized that the Holy Spirit was engaging me and wanted me to ask what this means. So, I did, and upon doing so, I was instantly drawn into a vision where I saw the peak of a huge mountain top. The Holy Spirit proceeded to tell me that a conqueror can't go any further than the mountain top because he conquered it, but when you are more than a conqueror, you are unbound, unrestricted and nothing can hold you back! The sky is the limit. I was carried away into another vision of a previous dream that I had from some time ago of me flying in the sky over towns and then towards a mountain of which I flew to the top, gasped, and flew back down. This encounter occurred in November 2018 right in the middle of my experience dealing with the trauma of church hurt which began in the fall of 2016. This encounter with the Holy Spirit soothed my weak spirit as I tried to navigate a series of events that I had never faced before. To be quite honest, before 2016, I was not familiar with the terminology of "church hurt" until it made its introduction to me. At the beginning of the trauma, I would often ask myself, what was wrong with me to have placed a target on my back.

Before the trauma beginning, my focus was on pressing into more of God in healing and miracles. I was desperate to see the kingdom of God demonstrated because of the vast amounts of people just from my own surroundings who were plagued with all manners of illnesses, and content about it. I began to review the scriptures on the early church, and Jesus himself and how the Kingdom of God was demonstrated, and this further stirred me to dig deeper in prayer and fasting.

While in prayer, the words of Jesus reverberated in my spirit when He said,

> " And these signs will follow those who believe: In My name they will cast out demons; they will speak with new tongues; they will take up serpents; and if they drink anything deadly, it will by no means hurt them; they will lay hands on the sick, and they will recover." (Mark 16:17-18)

During this moment, I asked the Father, "Where is the demonstration of your Kingdom in the church?" I took it a step further and examined myself, and exactly what I believed, or if I believed what the scriptures state about healing. My conclusion was that I am a believer, and I want to be a living reflection of what Jesus says that should be occurring. This was the genesis of my search, which led me to find books on people who walked under this anointing which further provoked me and caused me to view the scriptures with new understanding. This stirring and hunger set off a motion of events that changed me forever. I had the confidence to pray for the sick in faith and when this happened, people were getting healed! I began to witness legs growing out and backs coming into alignment, bodily lumps diminish just to name a few and all the glory given to God Himself. This was all exciting and new, so I continued to seek God diligently in prayer and fasting, wanting to be a willing and clean vessel. It was like I was a kid in the candy store. Then suddenly, during the fall of 2016, the first arrow of accusation was released, but not without warning.

Weeks before this arrow was released, I had a dream about a tornado approaching. The sky was dark, and I could see the tornado in the distance. I am originally from Oklahoma, which is known to be in the path of what meteorologists call "Tornado Alley," so seeing the tornado ahead in the dream brought on sheer dread in my emotions. I turned to go in the opposite direction, but the wind was strong and seemed to be holding me back. It was like I could not move ahead. When the arrow was released, the effects of the impact caused me to arrive at a place where I felt spiritually unable to move forward. The accusations were released on my husband as well because we both were in leadership positions. The attacks did not occur behind closed doors, but we were literally brought before the congregation and attacked openly on three different occasions. The first two times, this would happen to my husband because, on those days, I was otherwise occupied. However, looking back, I realize and believe that God was shielding me knowing that I would not be able to withstand those open attacks at first. The accusations consisted of us being labeled as prideful and offensive. During the last public attack, I was present, and as usual, was summoned to the front of the congregation and accused of having demon spirits. To add insult to injury, the scripture in 2 Timothy 5:20 which states:"

"Those who are sinning rebuke in the presence of all, that the rest also may fear," was used to justify what was taking place before the congregation with us. However, the scripture right before this in 2 Timothy 5:19 w aptly states:

"Do not receive an accusation against an elder except from two or three witnesses," was conveniently overlooked. We were always blindsided, and the accusations came out of seemingly nowhere and made no sense. Any attempts on our part to address what was occurring never produced any fruit as the parties involved stood their ground and never offered any sane reason for what was happening nor apologized for the false accusations. These experiences collectively took the air out of my body, and as stated earlier about the warning dream with the tornado, I felt my whole being come to a standstill because I could not understand why this was happening. This placed me on a path to a spiritual wilderness

as my foundation was shaken to its core because those that I looked up to for spiritual guidance seemed to have turned on my husband and myself most viciously and it devastated me.

The path towards healing from the trauma of church hurt was difficult and uncomfortable, to say the least. At this point, I became untrusting of any type of church leadership across all spectrums and wanted to shield and protect myself from any further hurt. The Holy Spirit had other plans, however, and deep down, I was tired of the emotional roller coaster that I seemed to be riding on and off. Sometime after this realization, and by the leading of the Holy Spirit, I was introduced to a ministry by a stranger that after praying for me, suggested that I attend some classes they offered on Tuesday evenings. Upon the person telling me this, I felt led to go, but not without hesitation because it was taking me out of my comfort zone. Nevertheless, I signed up immediately.

To summarize, my experience there caused me to be re-introduced to my identity in Jesus and be stripped of all the lies that up until this time was the counterfeit identity. During this stripping process, I realized that I was wearing the effects of the counterfeit identity that included shame, guilt, and condemnation. The leaders at this school were instrumental in demonstrating the heart of the Father and viewed me, a stranger, through the lens of Jesus. The Holy Spirit gently let me know to only wear what the Father gives and that was the garment of praise.

Attending each class caused another layer of pain to be released and I was being transformed. I came to know Jesus in a way that I had never experienced before and truly embraced what He said about me, and His thoughts towards me. Everything changed! I was no longer devastated by the words of men, and their opinions of me. The closing theme for the school of ministry for the year was appropriately titled: Who the Son sets Free Is Free Indeed! This newfound freedom was incredible!

The entire length of this experience of church hurt took place within three years from 2016 to 2019. While in prayer towards the end of this, the Holy Spirit showed me the significance of what I went through and to trust the timing of God. Throughout the three-year trial, I would still have dreams about healings and miracles but felt defeated due to the trauma and did not move forward. He pointed out that those three years were like the three trimesters that a woman experiences during pregnancy, and that delivery was going to take place. A full-term baby of course is delivered at 40 weeks. To continue to wreck me in a good way, the Holy Spirit pointed out the timing of my birthday at the end of this three-year ordeal where I would turn 40 years of age on February 2, 2020. What the enemy meant for evil, God was turning it around for my good! Delivery was taking place! My level of faith skyrocketed, and I felt a new strength arise within me that was solidly on Jesus.

Anyone who has ever experienced church hurt all has different stories and even different outcomes. One thing is for certain, trials will absolutely come but what is key is to be established in your identity in Jesus and embrace who He says that you are. You do not have to wear the effects of shame, guilt, and condemnation. This revelation can only come by true intimacy and cultivation of a relationship with Him. I can stand today knowing that I am fully healed, delivered, and set free from church hurt. I am a survivor of spiritual abuse, but my story does not end there. I am an OVERCOMER and MORE than a CONQUEROR!

Chapter 9

Overcomer's Written Interview

Name: Prophetess Dawn Akita Wellington
Ministry: Senior Pastor, Christ Church International Boston, MA
Email: ccibost@gmail.com

Have you experienced spiritual abuse and/or have you helped individuals who have? Please explain.

Yes, I have experienced spiritual abuse from my last church that I attended. My former pastor was a female pastor, whom I served under for six years. I believe that it was spiritual abuse based on the way that she treated certain people. She had her favorites and made it known that she had favorites. She believed that it was okay to make this known. She would explain that Jesus had a favorite, which was John, as the Bible says John was the one that He loved. She mistreated me and this caused me to feel some type of way so, I felt the Lord address me to work on myself. So I would buy her gifts and leave them in her office as my duties were to clean her office and church bathrooms. There were many incidents, but there was a particular time that she told me that she didn't like my gift and gave it back to me and told me to get her something different. This was very hurtful!

There was another time that she was teaching a class and she wanted me out of the class. I actually can't remember why. I really wanted to stay in the class, so she made me write ten pages of paper to do a write-up. And anytime it was time for me to speak in that class, she would have someone call her out. I know for a fact that it was deliberate. There was another time that she asked a member who is a friend of mine if I was going to hell would they go with me. I asked her about it with the person and she denied it, but the person said it to her face "Yes, you did say that to me and I did not like that". She later met with that person and rebuked them for confronting her and showing that she was a liar. These are only some of my experiences.

How did you recover from spiritual abuse? (Name 2 or 3 things that were instrumental in recovery)

I think forgiveness is definitely one and also knowing that the person is human. It has nothing to do with God with the way that they are acting. A lot of times when people treat us a certain way, they will relate it to "Oh, I'm not going to church anymore or I'm not going to sit under a woman leader because they are emotional, they are clingy or they have their cliques, or I'm not going to do this". We make our decisions based upon our relationship with God and church based on a person who is human and has flaws. There are reasons why people behave this way. Some people don't recover from it. But forgiveness helps you to understand that people are highly flawed.

What impact do you feel spiritual abuse has had on you to serve in your calling and purpose to date?

I would say if I see myself doing anything similar to what was done to me, it is to make sure that I correct it and to make sure I don't operate that way as far as bleeding. If anything like this would be brought to my attention or if I see it within myself, I would make sure that I tried my best to correct it.

What recommendations do you have for people who want to return to church but are afraid to trust again?

Definitely seek to find out what is the root of the problem. A lot of times we act certain ways because of what was done to us and we never deal with the root of the issue. Whether it is going back and talking to that person who spiritually abused you, maybe they don't know, maybe they do know. Forgiveness is not about them, it's about you. If it is something that you cannot do, pray for that person and ask and seek God to heal you from it. Because we have to realize that people have problems and issues regardless of their leadership title, they are still people, and everybody is going to need some form of deliverance from now until Jesus comes back. Just knowing that if you are dealing with people, you are dealing with people, no matter if they are titled or not.

What lessons have you learned that would inform better practices for church leadership?

If you are a Senior Leader, know that your members are the people that God has given to you. You have to act like a parent, so if you have ten kids or twenty kids, you should operate within the correct way of parenting. Every person should feel special, and no-one should feel unwanted. Deal with people according to their limits and barriers and let people know that you do care about them. Be sure to treat people the opposite of how you were treated when you were spiritually abused.

Overcomer's Written Interview

Name: DeShonda Monique Jennings
Organization: DJ It Takes A Village LLC
Website: www.ittakesavillage2.org
Email: dj@ittakesavillage2.com
Social Media: @djittakesavillage

DeShonda Monique Jennings is a wife, mother, grandma, and author. She grew up in a small rural town of Kenbridge, VA. DeShonda has a Bachelor's in Accounting with a Minor in Business Management and a degree in Early Childhood Development. She currently serves as an advocate and mentor for children as well as a mentor to women who wish to start a home daycare business. She is a firm believer in "It Takes a Village". She ran a successful home daycare for over 10 years. DeShonda is also a group cruise specialist. She offers discounts on travel at www.DeeJTravel.org.

Have you experienced spiritual abuse and/or have you helped individuals who have? Please explain.

In 2005, I experienced one of the biggest heartaches in my life. At the time, when I was brokenhearted and searching for answers in the church, I was introduced to a local ministry. I truly believed that I was doing the right thing by finding a church home and taking my whole family with me, which means my husband, my daughter, my son, and unborn child. I did everything that I thought was the right thing to bring me closer to God. What I mean by that was attend church on Sunday morning service and Sunday night service. I attended the weekly Bible study. I attended the weekly women's Bible study. I attended all the church events that happened every week. I even disenrolled my son and my daughter out of the public schools and enrolled them in the church school. Every time my pastors asked me to bring money to the altar, I did. There were times that I didn't have it but I still gave. It was stated to me that if we did not obey God, I would be condemned. It wasn't a huge congregation. A lot of the members in the church seem to hurt behind the smiles that they showed at the forefront. As I got deeper and deeper into this ministry, I didn't feel that God was healing me. I began to question myself and ask God is this my punishment for all the things that I have done in my past? Mind you, I came to the church for healing not to be hurt even more. Even in this ministry, the pastor and co-pastor began to tell me that my husband was of the devil. At this time, I had already been married for nine years.

In the beginning, my husband attended every service with me then as time went by, he wanted to stay home on Sunday nights and wanted me to leave the kids at home as well. My co-pastor told me that my husband was of the devil because he did not want to come back to church for the third service on a Sunday. I truly believed everything that they told me was correct. There was even a time when I needed gas money to get to work and I didn't have it and I reached out to a good friend of mine. My co-pastor had me call my friend back and let her know that I don't need the money. She also told me that everything that I needed was in the church. Attending this church for 6 to 7 months seemed like an eternity.

Once I joined the church, my relationship with my husband started to go downhill. My kids became very unhappy. I was told that I cannot allow my mother to watch my kids because she did not serve the God that we served. Also, during this time because I sold all my seeds into this ministry, we got evicted from my apartment; an apartment I was so proud to have before being evicted. My car got repossessed because I did not have the money to make my car payment since all my seeds were being sowed into the church. I also dropped out of school because I had no time to do my studies. I had to give up the second job that I loved so much because I enjoy working with the people. Once again, my co-pastor told me that two jobs were for two people. Like I said, I wanted to do everything that my Pastors told me so God would love me. I wanted to honor my Father. This is just a snippet of some of the spiritual abuse that I experienced.

How did you recover from spiritual abuse? (Name 2 or 3 things that were instrumental in your recovery)

There were a few key things that were instrumental in me recovering from spiritual abuse. To be honest, healing wasn't an easy process. I had to forgive them. Forgiveness isn't always something you want to do. In the beginning, I thought that they needed to ask me for forgiveness. I later learned that as long as I had unforgiveness in my heart, they still had control over me. When I truly forgave them, I felt a weight lifted. My life began to shift to a more positive and productive one. The second thing is I had to study God's word for myself. I had to learn and meditate on the written word. That way I could discern if someone were speaking into my life was in alignment with what God said for my life.

What impact do you feel spiritual abuse has had on you to serve in your calling and purpose to date?

Going through the season of spiritual abuse has now birthed me the voice and passion to mentor people by sharing my life experiences. My story gives hope to those who are going through similar situations. I was blessed to use my passion to start quality in-home daycare. My purpose is being filled through my organization DJ It Takes A Village LLC for I now know that God sends His angels to help and bless us.

What recommendations do you have for people who want to return to church but are afraid to trust again?

> *"Now ye are the body of Christ, and members in particular."* 1 Corinthians 12:27, KJV

First of all, I would say that we are the church. The church is not the building. As of the date of writing this chapter, I do not have a membership in a particular church building. One of the things that I did was, I visited several different Church buildings to hear the pastor deliver the word. By doing so, I was able to hear if the word resonated with me as well as if the message was what was in the Bible. I'm saying not to make a quick decision to become a member. The following scripture helped me to obtain this. *"Do not be anxious about anything, but in every situation, by prayer and petition, with thanksgiving, present your requests to God. And the peace of God, which transcends all understanding, will guard your hearts and your minds in Christ Jesus."* Philippians 4:6-7 Therefore, do not be afraid.

What lessons have you learned that would inform better practices for church leadership?

Be a servant leader. Leadership is key. Don't fall for the "do as I say, not as I do" when it comes to leadership. Leaders set the example of what life looks like according to God's will. Leaders will be able to help those that they are called to serve. Leaders will give specific instructions and directions according to God's written word. Leaders will help you understand who you are and whose you are.

About the Author

Mercy Myles-Jenkins was born and raised in London, England, by Ghanaian parentage. She currently resides in Massachusetts with her family.

Mercy is an ordained pastor of Christ Church International Springfield, an apostolic-prophetic church. Mercy believes that 'Spiritual Health is Mental Health,' and that as the Church, we need to take responsibility to support those who have been affected by it's malpractices.

Mercy is a certified Life Coach and supports women to overcome spiritual abuse through coaching. Mercy has written 5 books on overcoming Spiritual Abuse and in that process, she became a Book Coach with a successful Book Coaching program. Mercy started her company Legacy Driven Consulting & Publishing, as a mission to inspire and equip women to build their legacy by leading with their story in a book. Mercy empowers women to emerge from being invisible to evolve as they learn to find their voice to make an impact.

Bibliography

1. Myles-Jenkins M, 'God's Mercy in the Wilderness: A Guide to Finding Your Calling & Purpose in the Midst of Church Hurt', 2017
2. Eckhardt, John. 'Prayers That Rout Demons & Break Curses'. Charisma House, 2010.
3. Virkler, Mark, and Patti Virkler. "Prayers That Heal the Heart." Prayers That Heal the Heart, Bridge Logos Foundation, 2007
4. Myles-Jenkins M, 'Run for Your Life', 2020
5. Myles-Jenkins M, 'Uncovering the Betrayal of Spiritual Abuse', 2020
6. https://psychologydictionary.org/self-confidence/

Mercy
MYLES-JENKINS
Author/Speaker/Real Estate Investor
Grab Your Copy Today!
Tel: (413) 351-8154
Purpose Pusher
President: New England Branch,
Women With A Call International
www.CoachMercyMylesJenkins.com

For More Information, please go to
www.CoachMercyMylesJenkins.com

Made in the USA
Middletown, DE
25 November 2020